1

*Valuable lessons on leadership, service, mentoring and philanthropy
shared within the pages of a story that speaks directly to teens*

Dana Lara, High School Student

-

An incredibly inspiring story of perseverance and kindness

Marina Paul, 5th Grade Teacher

-

A virtual case study for First Year Experience programs

Amy Pszczolkowski, Asnuntuck Community College

-

*Demonstrates the power within each of us to spark positive change
...helps middle schoolers view the world from a different perspective*

Theresa Taylor, Middle School Assistant Principal

-

*A remarkable story of strength filled with lessons that will
take every student through the college years and beyond*

College News

-

...shows what is possible when we include others at our table

Lenard Zohn, Founder, Autism Eats

-

*A lesson in humanity...a positive message that is particularly
relevant to high school students but valuable to everyone*

Midwest Book Review

-

*The story of a man who treats life as art – and created
a masterpiece by helping others realize their dreams*

Art World News

-

*A memorable example of the magical bond between
kids with big dreams and the grandparents who believe in them*

Brenda Tripp-Lanser, Director, Monroe Public Library

To the overlooked and the underestimated.
To the parents, grandparents,
teachers, mentors and substitute teachers
who encourage people to dream.
- JNP

———

*"If life was nothing but straight lines,
it wouldn't be worth living."*
- Greg's Grandma

———

15th *Anniversary Edition*

THE FIRST THIRTY
as told to Jillip Naysinthe Paxson
by Greg Forbes Siegman

www.TheFirstThirty.com

2007 Northeast Student Diversity Leadership Conference
Multicultural Relations Book of the Year

There are other versions of this story for audiences
of different ages & reading levels – as well as –
a companion journal workbook based on this story.
For more on those books and that workbook, visit
www.GregForbes.com/books

THE FIRST THIRTY
as told to Jillip Naysinthe Paxson by Greg Forbes Siegman

ISBN: 978-0-9758794-8-1
Library of Congress Control Number: 2020903923

About the Cover: Photo by Pam Siegman
Concept by IdeaList Enterprises Inc.

Introduction

Tempo Cafe
November 10, 2002 – 11:48 P.M.

Why did Greg choose someone with no writing experience to share his story?

It's a fair question.

Here's an honest answer: life isn't always fair.

The fact of the matter is that only one person on the list of people hoping to tell his story used to play catch with him in his yard twenty-five years ago. And that would be me.

Given that I've known Greg since I was little, you might wonder why I need to interview him before sharing his story with you. We were childhood friends. I should know his story, right?

Well, the fact is our old bond is exactly that – an *old* bond.

The last time we saw each other, we were kids throwing that ball around the yard. The connection was enough to help get me chosen to write the story, but it isn't enough to make me an expert on it.

Let's face it. I knew Greg when he wet himself on a regular basis. What are the chances the boy I knew and the man he has become are remotely the same? I doubted I'd even recognize the guy.

But to my surprise, when he walked through the door, I spotted him right away. It was actually easy. I mean, who else but Greg shows up at a restaurant with a lunchbox in one hand and a gold-painted milkshake glass in the other?

Not that I gave either item much thought. After he spoke briefly with the manager standing by the cash register, he walked over to the table and joined me. At that moment, I got a good look at my old friend and forgot all about what he was holding.

The same boy who ran around the backyard until the sun went down now walked delicately – like a banged-up athlete trying to avoid any sudden movement after the game. His skin was pale and lifeless, and he needed a shave. The bags under his eyes looked out of place on the face of a thirty year old – except that they matched the bags above them. The eyes themselves, once described in a magazine as 'penetrating', looked worn and tired – as if they spent far too many nights fighting to stay open.

His shirt and pants were wrinkled and at least two sizes too big (in a he-must-have-lost-fifteen-pounds-since-he-bought-them kind of way). His thick mop of brown hair was even gone – replaced by, well, nothing.

During a brief chat on the phone a few days ago, he said, "If you don't recognize me when I walk in, look for the big ears."

At the time, I figured he was joking. When he sat down at the table, I realized he was not. His ears really did seem to be the only thing that had not changed since he was little.

I started to ask the first question on my mind – *What happened to you?* – but before I could get out the words, he offered seven of his own.

"Mind if I take off my shoes?"

Before I could reply, he already had leaned over to remove them – revealing two mismatched socks in the process.

"Sorry, we're meeting so late," he said, as he rubbed his left foot. "I had a movie to see tonight."

I was anxious to shift my focus from his startling appearance and begin the interview. This seemed like a good topic to break the ice.

"What film did you see?"

He laughed and said, "You want *that* to be your one question?"

"Excuse me?" I asked.

"Did I forget to mention that?" Greg asked, as he fiddled with his ears. "You're only allowed to ask me one question."

"Says who?" I protested.

"Says me," he replied.

At first, I figured he was kidding. He couldn't possibly expect me to get all the information I needed to write an entire book by asking a single question. And yet, judging by the look on Greg's face, it was clear that he was serious.

I could not believe what I was hearing. I spent weeks preparing for the interview. I agreed to his odd request that we meet at this unlikely hour in this unlikely location to have the meeting. Now, after all that, I could only ask one question?

For a moment, a sense of helplessness got the best of me.

"I can't do it," I said with a shrug. "I give up."

"Oh, come on," he pleaded. "You can't give up *that* easy."

Despite my frustration, I chuckled a little. It was exactly like when we were little. He wanted to outsmart me – to dream up riddles that I couldn't solve – but I ruined his fun if I gave up too quickly.

"Fine," I said with a smile, "but I have to think about this for a second. It's not too easy reducing thirty years to one question."

Naturally, my first instinct was to ask him about the chapter of his life for which he was known best. That fateful day six years ago when he witnessed a moment of intolerance at a restaurant and rose from his seat to do something about it – determined to be more than a bystander.

I quickly overruled myself.

Yes, that was an important part of his story – even the President of the United States at the time expressed support for what resulted from Greg's actions in that restaurant that day – but I wanted to dig deeper. Instead of just telling a one-dimensional, feel-good story about a person who made a difference, I wanted to paint a more complete picture. I wanted to write about the people, places and experiences that shaped his path and his efforts. I also wanted to write about the missteps and mistakes he made during the process – because that is usually when we learn the best lessons.

While the waitress came over and took his order – a vanilla milkshake and a grilled cheese sandwich – I sat quietly and thought about his riddle. What one question could get you all the information you need to write a book about the first thirty years of someone's life and the people who impacted him along the way?

I couldn't think of a good one off the top of my head, but I knew that with most problems in life, as long as you don't get too frustrated and quit, the solution will eventually come to you.

Sure enough, that's what happened in this case. By the time Greg had his meal, I had my question.

"Okay," I said, while he carefully dipped the tip of his straw into the shake to measure its thickness like a young child using his big toe to check the temperature of the water in a pool. "I've come up with my question."

"Yeah?" he replied, as he nibbled on his sandwich. "Let's hear it."

"Will you start at the beginning?"

Judging by the smile on his face, I apparently solved the riddle.

As the clock struck midnight and the first thirty years of his life came to an end, Greg sat up straight, wiped a couple crumbs off his face, cleared his throat and did as I asked.

He started at the beginning.

**

THE BEGINNING

On November 10, 1972, a 30 year old Army Veteran-turned-stockbroker named Mark and his wife, Rose, had their first child.

The boy's first name, Gregory, was chosen in memory of a late relative (whose first name started with a G). The middle name, Forbes, was thought up by Mark in honor of billionaire Malcolm Forbes and *Forbes* magazine. Mark had never actually met the famous businessman, but he hoped the name would inspire his son to the same level of success.

The young couple was excited to have their first child. Rose spent hour after hour, day after day, watching and caring for their new baby boy. Mark did the same after returning home from work each night.

A year later, they had a baby girl. They intended to divide their time evenly between their two kids, but that plan quickly changed – and with good reason. Their daughter was gravely ill.

For the better part of a year, Rose practically lived by her baby's side at the hospital. Mark joined them each night after spending the day at work.

In the meantime, with his parents so focused on his new sister's health, Greg was usually dropped off at his Grandma's. Given his age, the two didn't have any real conversations, but as she rocked him back and forth on her lap, an unspoken bond did seem to develop between them.

Thanks to some amazing doctors, Greg's little sister eventually pulled through, things got back to 'normal' and the family of four moved into a two story home on a quiet, little street in the suburbs.

The three bedrooms were upstairs – one for Greg, one for his sister and one for their parents. Greg's window overlooked the backyard – a square of grass and bushes enclosed by a white fence. In the far corner, across from Greg's window, there was jungle gym equipment. One piece was a giant horse standing on its hind legs. Its back was a ladder that could be climbed up and down. The other piece was a fifteen foot tall, multi-colored stick figure man with his arms stretched out, a swing hanging from each arm.

At night, the man's colors were draped by the darkness – turning him into a towering silhouette rising up into the sky.

Sometimes, Greg swung on The Silhouette Man's swings or climbed the Horse's ladder. Most days, though, he was content to sit in the grass, watch the Man and the Horse, and wait for the moment when they finally *moved.*

Greg's belief that The Ladder Horse and The Silhouette Man could move like real people was the tip of the iceberg when it came to his imagination. In fact, the boy spent so much time day-dreaming – and got so distracted by ideas floating through his head – that he ran into things.

At one point, his father even gave him a helmet to wear around the house, so he stopped hurting his head when he bumped into the walls.

When Mark came home from work each night, the family sat down in the kitchen for dinner. It was never much of a unified event. Greg's parents and his sister ate one thing. He always ate another.

No matter how hard anyone tried to convince him otherwise, Greg stubbornly insisted on eating only six things: hot dogs without mustard, peanut butter without jelly, bagels without lox, French toast without syrup, cereal with milk (but only as long as the milk was in a separate glass so he could eat the cereal with his hands) and grilled cheese sandwiches (which he insisted on calling *meatless cheeseburgers*).

And that was it. Every single meal, every single day, it had to be one of those six things. (Greg's mom did have one small victory. Hoping to put some weight on her frail son, she convinced him vanilla milkshakes were filled with special paint that kept teeth bright and shiny).

Once Greg started school, it did not take long for the older kids to make fun of his eating habits, but it was hardly the only thing they mocked. Right off the bat, he was teased about the way he looked.

He had buck teeth and the kind of chubby cheeks that led people to believe he was hiding gumballs in his mouth. He also had enormous ears – the kind normally seen in cartoons. He tried to comb his hair over them or hide them under hats, but nothing ever worked. Sooner or later, they always managed to pop back out.

And then there was that middle name. Forbes wasn't like John or David. It was different. Greg's parents said it was different in a good way, but their claim did not sway him. To Greg, it was one more thing on a never-ending list of things that people teased him about. He eventually pretended he had no middle name at all.

To top it off, whenever he got nervous, he peed on himself.

He was an easy target for teasing if there ever was one.

Despite Greg's problems, there was one thing that did go his way. His teachers. Year after year, he had some of the nicest ones a kid could hope for. They were kind and patient and never teased him about anything (or let anyone else tease him in front of them, either). Other than his bedroom and the backyard, the classroom quickly became his favorite place to be.

That's not to say the teasing stopped completely. Before and after school, when the teachers weren't there to protect him, Greg still had to fend for himself against the older kids.

As the weeks passed, he appreciated the peace and quiet of his backyard more than ever. It became his private hiding spot. The one place he could go outside without having to worry about running into the older kids who picked on him. Before long, the jungle gym equipment out back – the man-shaped swing set and the horse-shaped ladder – became his *friends*. Greg talked to them for hours at a time.

(In later years, people teased Greg for talking too much – unaware it could be traced directly to the fact that, as a child, he spent hours carrying on conversations with two 'friends' who never said a word.)

When Mark found out his son talked to the jungle gym equipment, he was none too pleased. Hoping to see Greg put his time to better use, he gave him a smock and a brush and said, "Instead of talking to the ladder and the swing set, why don't you paint some pictures of them?"

Greg did as his father told him, but the results were not too impressive. No matter how hard he tried, he could barely draw a straight line. He was on the verge of giving up when his Grandma stepped in.

"You're right, you stink at art," she said in her no-nonsense way, "but so what? You learn more from your mistakes than you learn when you get it right. All that matters is you don't give up. If life was nothing but straight lines, it wouldn't be worth living."

He followed her advice – and not only with drawing. When he first tried to read, the sentences got all scrambled up in his head. Instead of giving up, he kept trying. Over time, the words fell in place. It was an experience that shaped one of the first lessons of Greg's young life.

(1) Work twice as much as the people you think are twice as smart and eventually, you'll catch up.

Once Greg learned to read, he never wanted to stop. He read in the morning before anyone woke up. He read after his mom tucked him in at night, too – hiding beneath his covers with a flashlight. On weekends, he stayed at the public library for as long as it was open.

Oh, how he loved that library!

The people he read about, the things they did and the places they went filled his imagination with ideas and carried him far away from the 'real' world where he never felt quite like he belonged.

Of the books he read, one of his favorites was a book about a pro athlete. Greg wanted to be one, too. He ran around the yard, wearing that football helmet his parents gave him. He played imaginary games against imaginary friends. Until, finally, his father decided he was old enough to play real games with real people. He signed Greg up for tee ball (which is when he first became friends with a kid named Charlie).

Shel Silverstein's books of poetry captured Greg's attention, too. With a different poem every few pages, they were a perfect fit for a boy who got so easily distracted.

The Little Engine That Could was a book he liked to read over and over. The story shared the same message his Grandma emphasized: Don't Quit.

Greg also loved *Where the Wild Things Are.* The popular book told the story of a boy who is magically transported to another land with giant creatures. After reading the story, Greg became convinced The Silhouette Man and The Ladder Horse in his backyard could come to life – no matter what anyone said about them being mere metal and paint. At night, he sat in bed and stared at them outside his window – watching and waiting for the moment they moved like other real people do.

Greg's favorite book was about Harriet Tubman – partly because it was the first book he ever bought himself (at a grade school book fair) and partly because he was so inspired by her commitment to helping people.

The son of a white, suburban businessman growing up in the 1970's obviously could not really understand what it was like for a black woman to live through slavery and then further risk her life to help more people escape slavery a hundred years earlier. Nevertheless, in his own little-kid-kind-of-way, Greg aspired to be like Harriet. He wanted to help people, too.

A few weeks later, a visitor came to his school and talked about a program where kids help fight a disease called Multiple Sclerosis by getting people to donate money for every book they read. He eagerly signed up.

Rose was not quite as excited. The Read-a-Thon program seemed tailor-made for her book-loving son, and she knew it was a nice charity. But she feared Greg was too shy to approach people and ask them to donate money for every book he read.

As it turned out, the program served as a great way to bring the boy out of his shell. Determined to make a difference, he set aside his insecurity, laced up his shoes, walked all over town and knocked on neighbors' doors. He asked everyone he knew and everyone he met to make a pledge.

Despite his age and inexperience, he proved to be very good at doing it. He persuaded some people to give a one-time donation (like, twenty dollars). Others pledged a certain amount for every book he read – usually a few cents per book – which motivated him to read more than ever.

While other kids finished a book a week, Greg knocked out one a day. At the age of six, he was raising hundreds of dollars.

It was the first time he felt like he did something well. He was a milkshake-slurping, book-reading, fund-raising machine. By the time he was eight, the total he raised was in the thousands.

Many people noticed Greg's efforts. The charity honored him at a luncheon. The newspaper ran his picture with the headline *Champ Reader*. His favorite TV star, Fonzi, sent a kind note and autographed photo. NFL players even took time to meet with him and encourage him to keep reading.

For a kid accustomed to being teased, the positive support was a great feeling. The more lasting reward was what he learned from the process of sitting in his room and at the library and reading all those books:

(2) Anyone at any age can make a difference.
All you need is time and the willingness to spend it.

There seemed to be nothing that made Greg happier than reading those books and raising that money. Until, one day, his mom took him to the theater where his godfather worked and introduced him to a whole new universe – the world of movies.

At first, the darkness of the theater scared him. Then, he realized it was a blessing. Thanks to the lack of lighting, most of the other people in the audience did not notice him. As a result, the theater became another place he could go without much fear of being teased.

Not that it really mattered. Once the previews played, he forgot about everyone and everything around him. The wall had come to life, and he was positively hypnotized!

He returned to the theater regularly. He watched the movies over and over. At home, he watched old films playing on TV or video, too.

All day long, Greg imitated characters. He ran up the stairs like he was Rocky, the boxer in *Rocky*, training for a match. He paced in front of The Silhouette Man swing set in the backyard like he was Atticus, the lawyer in *To Kill a Mockingbird*, talking to the judge.

Rose was amused by Greg's antics, but his father was not. Concerned that his son still could not tell fiction from reality, Mark asked Greg's godfather to take the boy up to the projectionist's booth at the movie theater. He asked him to show Greg the machine that makes the film appear on the screen and to explain how the wall doesn't really come to life.

Greg's godfather did as asked. Unfortunately for Mark, his plan to take the magic out of movie-making backfired. The concept of one man in a little booth running the entire show left Greg more awe-struck than the films themselves. It was like a modern day *Wizard of Oz*.

From that day forward, he still hoped to be like the people he saw on screen. But if he never did become strong like Rocky or become a lawyer like Atticus, he now had a new dream to fill the void. He wanted to be the one who told their stories.

As time went on, Greg continued to insist *that* was his destiny. He was going to be the one who told the stories that played on the screen. One day, he insisted, he would tell stories about underdogs like *Rocky*, about people who stuck up for others like *To Kill a Mockingbird*, and about places where it was okay to dream like *Willy Wonka and the Chocolate Factory.*

He vowed, "I'll tell stories that change the way people think."

He said his stories would be so good that he would win an Academy Award ® for his first one. Night after night, while his family sat around the dinner table in the kitchen, he lifted up his glass like it was a trophy and practiced the first six words of his acceptance speech over and over again.

"I'd like to thank the Academy…"

**

Between the films, the books and his friends in the backyard, Greg seemed increasingly happy in his own little world and increasingly lost in the real one. If he had even thirty seconds to himself, his mind drifted off in a dozen different directions.

Within ten minutes of learning how to ride a ten speed bike, he got distracted, crashed, went sailing through the handle bars and cut his head wide open. On a family vacation in California, he ran through the hotel lobby and out the front door – except that the door was closed and he went flying backwards. He got a bump on the front of his head from the collision and a bump on the back from the landing.

Time and time again, he got so distracted by what was going on in his head that he ran nose-first right into something.

(By the time he turned sixteen, he already cracked his head open twice and broke his nose four times – requiring two operations. Some of the injuries were the result of sports, but more often than not, they were caused by distractions.)

As time went on, Mark tried to get his son to ignore the adventures going on inside his head, but it was easier said than done. Everywhere Greg looked in the real world, there seemed to be something to fear.

Even on his own street, where all the neighbors and their kids treated him nicely, he still found plenty of excuses to be afraid. Three houses to the left, there lived a girl with pretty blue eyes. Whenever Greg saw her, he stuttered. Three doors to the right, there lived a giant dog who always seemed like he was about to pounce. Whenever Greg saw the dog or heard it growl, he peed on himself.

Sometimes, Greg played catch with the boy who lived in the house next door. Other times, on weekends, he slept over at the houses of some of the other kids his age. Many nights, though, he preferred to put up a tent in his backyard and stay up late talking with his two loyal friends, The Silhouette Man and The Ladder Horse.

At home, he felt safe. At least, he did until the burglar broke in.

One night, Greg came face-to-face with a man who broke into the house. The man ran back down the stairs and out the door as soon as he was spotted, but Greg still trembled with fear two full hours later. His parents tried to convince him there had been no burglar.

"It was your shadow," they told him.

It was no use. The damage was already done. Night after night, Greg insisted on sleeping in his parents' room. He was terrified the burglar would come back to get him. When four weeks passed and he was still afraid to be alone, his dad decided he had enough. Determined to reclaim his domain, Mark surprised Greg with something that could keep him company at night – his very own dog.

The idea worked. Even though the eight-week-old puppy was tiny, Greg felt like he now had a 'bodyguard'. He finally felt safe returning to his room.

As the days passed, Greg and the pup, whom he named Tug (after his favorite baseball player) became glued at the hip. After school, they watched TV together. At dinner, Tug sat loyally by Greg's feet. At night, Tug slept on the edge of Greg's bed. Nothing could pull the two apart.

Over the next few months, Tug grew rapidly. By summer, the little puppy was a full-fledged dog. With such a big friend to protect him, Greg felt safe inside the house. He finally felt safe outside, too. He roamed the neighborhood, smiling and happy and free – always with his trusty companion by his side.

Until, one day, seven short months after they met, Tug was gone.

It was a Saturday afternoon in July. Greg's Little League teammates and their families were over at the house for a backyard barbecue. When one of the kids opened the front door, Tug dashed outside and ran down the street. Three blocks later, he was hit by a car and killed.

It was the first time Greg lost a friend to violence. He was heartbroken. With tears streaming down his cheeks, he turned to his dad and asked him to explain how something like this could happen.

Greg's dad put his hand on his shoulder and said, "Sometimes, friends come into each other's lives. Then, when you least expect it, they move on. There's no real explanation for it. So, instead of trying to figure out why they left, you should appreciate them while they're here and make sure to remember them once they've gone."

Mark's comments became the basis for another lesson.

(3) Approach everyone you meet like they came into your life for a reason.

Mark's words helped Greg deal with the tragedy. It also gave the boy comfort to know Tug's ashes were buried behind three small bushes in the backyard, where he could keep an eye on them from his bedroom window.

Still, he was not the same without his best friend by his side. Weeks turned into months. Greg felt as sad and lonely as the day Tug died.

Hoping that time away from home helped their son put the tragedy behind him, Rose and Mark signed Greg up for overnight camp in Wisconsin. His pal, Charlie, was signed up by his parents, too.

At first, as he boarded the bus, even with Charlie there, Greg was afraid to spend eight weeks away from home with so many strangers. After a few days, though, he decided summer camp was one of the greatest places ever.

The boy from the white picket fence suburbs was no outdoorsman, but the chance to shoot a bow and arrow, run in the woods and swim in the lake was the closest thing he ever experienced to the adventurous world inside his head. He also appreciated that most everyone there went out of their way to treat him nicely. Even though Greg seemed 'different', the other kids in his cabin tried to make him feel like he was part of the group. The counselors were supportive, too. When Greg was nervous about trying new things, they were there to encourage him.

The Camp Director was especially thoughtful. When he heard about Greg's eating habits, he made sure there was always a cheese sandwich waiting – in case his finicky camper didn't eat what was being served. When Mark sent up a box of weight gain powder to mix in his skinny son's shakes, the Director let Greg drink the shakes in his office – to make sure the boy didn't feel self-conscious about it in front of the other kids.

At a party with a girls' camp, Greg even got his first kiss.

He returned to camp in Wisconsin every summer until he could drive.

When Greg came home from camp that first year, his parents were thrilled. Their son was going outside again and playing with his friends again. He even rambled about his dreams again.

Knowing how easily he got distracted, his Grandma encouraged him to write down those dreams on paper. As always, he followed her instructions.

When a dream crossed his mind, he wrote it down. Then, one day, he picked the ones he cared about most and put them in a list. He entitled it *My Idea List: The First Thirty.* It was the thirty goals, ideas and dreams that he hoped to reach by the time he was thirty years old. *The First Thirty* included many of the typical dreams for a boy of Greg's age. He wanted to go on a date with his blue-eyed neighbor. He dreamed of writing a best-selling book, traveling the world and winning his first argument in the Supreme Court. He also wanted to be a pro athlete and President of the United States (which he later changed to 'live in the White House' once he remembered you can't run the country until you're 35).

And on and on his 'Idea List' went.

He took the time to list the goals alphabetically. So, it was only a coincidence the first one happened to be the one he dreamed about most: *An Academy Award for his first film.*

Greg's parents were not surprised by the list of wide-eyed dreams that their son put together. Most of them were things he talked about for years.

They knew most of the goals were *so* big that he would probably never reach them – at least, not until he was much older. But mixed in with Greg's far-off dreams, there was one goal on the list that seemed a little more reachable in the near future: *Going to the Ivy Leagues for college.*

Mind you, Greg didn't know anything about Harvard, Princeton or the other schools that were in the elite group. He didn't know where they were located, or what their campuses looked like, or what classes they offered, or which professors taught there.

Truth be told, he didn't care, either. In fact, it didn't even matter to him if a school was actually in the Ivy Leagues. His sole focus was a school's reputation. All he cared about was attending a school known for only admitting 'really smart' students. If he could get into a school like that – if he could become *one of them* – he was certain the teasing would stop once and for all.

Of course, he couldn't attend one of those schools unless one of them accepted him. That led to the big question on his mind. Could he get in?

Deep down, he wasn't so sure.

Then, one day, he saw a movie that changed everything.

In the film, Princeton accepted a kid named Joel – even though he broke the law in front of one of the school's representatives. Once he saw that, Greg became certain he could get in, too. After all, Joel committed a crime. Just about the worst thing Greg ever did was put his feet on his Grandma's couch. How could he *not* get in?

He seemed to have a good point, except that Joel didn't actually exist. The guy was a made-up character in a made-up movie. Of course, there was no telling Greg that. If it happened in a book or movie, he believed it could happen in real life.

Over the next few years, Greg began his pursuit of the thirty goals that he called *The First Thirty.* Most of the goals he set were such grand ones that he fell flat on his face trying to reach them. A part of him wanted to rip up the list like it never existed, but his Grandma urged him not to do so.

"Don't you remember anything I ever taught you?" she huffed. "It's okay to get knocked down once in a while. If life was nothing but straight lines, it wouldn't be worth living."

It was an important lesson to remember, and the timing could not have been better. Greg was about to face a daunting new challenge.

High school.

**

From the start, Mortimer Dowhill Crest Randolph High School was a struggle for Greg. For the most part, he had only himself to blame.

The teachers assured him that he was doing well, but he never seemed willing to believe them. He worked himself into a panic over each and every assignment. The early progress reports to his parents almost always said the same thing: *Your son is a gifted student. I wish he realized it.*

Outside of class, he had his share of problems, too.

As one of MDCR's only Jewish students, Greg endured anti-Semitic remarks for the first time. It only happened a few times – a glimpse of what people who deal with intolerance on a daily basis must face – but as far as he was concerned, even one comment like that was one too many.

Knowing that he was too small to force someone to stop saying such things, Greg figured his only option was to avoid the guys making the comments. His Grandma insisted there was another choice.

She said, "Some of those fellas are probably repeating what they heard other people say and have no idea what those words mean. They're probably not bad kids – just stupid. You explain to them how offensive those words are. If any of them will listen to you, then maybe they will stop. And if they don't, well, at least you gave them the extra benefit of the doubt."

Greg reluctantly did as instructed. He asked the bullies if he could talk to them. As he predicted, they mostly ignored his request, but one guy was willing to hear what Greg had to say. After listening, he confessed that he knew he was being mean, but he had no idea that the words he used were as hurtful as they were. Now that someone explained it, he promised to stop.

After hearing how it turned out, Grandma nodded her approval and said, "Maybe, only one guy stopped, but the one who did, he isn't gonna just stop calling you those names and using those words. I'll bet he won't make fun of anyone else's religion, either."

(4) If you treat intolerance as hatred and avoid it,
you may be less likely to endure it again. If you treat it as ignorance
and try to address it, others may be less likely to endure it at all.

By the end of the year, things at school got a whole lot better for Greg. Over the course of nine months, he found that the benefits of having so many diverse peers were well worth the discomfort caused by one or two classmates making insensitive comments to him.

He was doing well academically, too. Despite his early self-doubts, he continued to work hard and ranked number one in the entire class. Away from the textbooks, he pursued his interest in writing through the school newspaper and its literary magazine. He also joined the cross country, baseball and basketball teams, took part in Junior Achievement and was elected Vice President of the class by his peers.

Everything seemed to be going smoothly, but it did not take long for him to hit another roadblock – *literally.*

All summer, he worked as a busboy to earn enough money to buy a car (his father matched one dollar for every dollar he earned).

In the fall, he got his license and showed off his new automobile around town. Until, less than two days later, he got distracted (as usual), had a horrible accident and the front of the car went up in flames.

Working and working to reach a goal, only to come crashing to the ground as he was starting to celebrate his success. It would be a metaphor for the story of Greg's life, and the source of the next lesson:

(5) No matter how far you've come,
always keep your eyes focused on the road ahead.

The crash was not the only setback during his second year at MDCR. One weekend, Greg found himself in a neighborhood where he'd never been. He was attacked by a group of a half-dozen young men.

In the days that followed, not wanting to talk at length about the terrible experience and keep reliving the memory, he stuck with the same brief summary when people asked about his bruises and bandages.

"A gang of thugs beat me up," he said to each of them.

When people heard that explanation, some of them said the incident was a reflection on *all* black people.

The remarks upset Greg almost as much as the incident itself. He knew racially charged issues could be complex, but this one seemed very straightforward for two reasons.

As Greg put it, "First of all, if a guy with dark hair does something bad, it doesn't mean all guys with dark hair are bad. If it's a guy with dark skin, why would it be any different? Those comments are stupid."

It was a good point, but he knew his second point did an even better job of revealing the ignorance of the comments that these people made.

The guys who beat him up were not black.

People heard the phrase 'gang of thugs' and had made an assumption.

In the weeks that followed, one small positive thing did come out of the unfortunate event. Greg finally started lifting weights.

His dad urged him to do so for a long time, and Greg did want to get bigger, but he was *so* skinny that he always had been afraid that he'd get laughed out of the gym if he dared to step inside.

After getting beat up, though, he no longer cared whether he was teased in the weight room. This was about self-defense. He needed to get bigger.

As it turned out, once he did go to the gym, nobody there laughed at all. In fact, most of the older, stronger guys went out of their way to help him. They taught him how to use the weights and offered encouragement. The finicky eater even expanded his diet and started eating more types of food after one of them took the time to explain how nutrition and exercise go hand in hand.

When Greg admitted he was surprised by how nicely they treated a younger, skinny kid, one of the bodybuilder types patted him on the back and said, "We all started somewhere."

*(6) Whether it is people or places, you need to look beyond the surface
if you really want to know what they're like inside.*

Greg was excited to have a new circle of friends from the health club, but he still couldn't stop thinking about the assault that led him there in the first place. From his perspective, it was another example that proved he had to overcome more setbacks than most – that his life wasn't fair.

Mark had mixed emotions about the situation. On the one hand, he felt badly Greg was beat up. On the other hand, he took it as a personal insult when his pampered son complained about his supposedly 'tough' life.

Mark said, "Sure, Greg faced setbacks, but everybody does. There were kids whose lives were a thousand times tougher than his. I provided a good life for him, and I felt it was time he realized that. So, I introduced him to Kahzti."

Kahzti grew up in an unsafe part of the world. At a young age, his parents snuck him onto a boat and, they hoped, on a voyage to a better life.

When Kahzti arrived in America – a teenager all alone in a foreign land – he was lonely, broke and didn't know the language. Yet, he somehow managed to scrape up enough money to get by, learn English and finish high school ranked at the top of his class.

Mark heard about Kahzti and had such respect for what he achieved that he cut a check to help pay the young man's college tuition. Now, Mark hoped Kahzti would give Greg another kind of check – a reality check.

The idea worked. After meeting Kahzti and hearing about his struggles, Greg knew he had no business complaining about the supposed 'obstacles' in his own life.

(7) One way to put your problems in perspective is to spend time with someone who can only dream their life is so easy.

Greg returned to school in the fall more determined than ever to reach his goals. By year's end, in and out of class, he was thriving.

He was an appointed Student Leader, a varsity athlete, re-elected to class office, an editor for the school paper and editor-in-chief of the literary magazine. In his free time, he lifted weights and coached a team in the Little League he played in as a boy. Other than Art (as much as he enjoyed trying to draw, he still could not do it well), his GPA was nearly perfect.

In his mind, his acceptance at Ivy League-level schools had gone from a fantasy to a certainty. With the lessons of the past few summers on his mind, though, he refused to slack off. To the contrary, he decided to work even harder – using his final year of high school as a chance to test himself and try new things.

One of those challenges he vowed to tackle was varsity football.

After drinking all those milkshakes with the weight-gain powder, spending all those hours lifting weights in the gym and finally eating more kinds of food, he filled out his six foot frame. Now that he had, the young man who used to run around the backyard pretending he was a football star wanted to play for real.

A few weeks before his senior year of high school, to get ready for the upcoming season, Greg took an all-day bus ride to Knox to attend a four day football camp with hundreds of other players from dozens of other high

schools around the country. Despite his fond memories of summers in
Wisconsin, Greg was nervous as he boarded the bus. Once again, though,
camp turned out to be an unforgettably fun experience.

On the field, he proved to be a quick study. He was named one of the
camp's All-Stars during closing ceremonies. Off the field, he made a new
friend. On the surface, Greg and Bailey seemed very different, but that's all
most of their differences were – on the surface. Despite coming from
different faiths, races and backgrounds, they had a lot in common.

The two hit it off right away and stayed in touch after camp ended. It
seemed to be the beginning of a new friendship.

For Greg, the season itself got off to a great start, too.

He scored a touchdown in his first game and a 90 yard TD in his second.
The team didn't win any championships, but the chance to be part of it felt
like a victory for a kid teased for so long about his size.

By December, he felt on top of the world. He was one semester shy of
graduation and had submitted all of his college applications.

He packed his bags for winter vacation, happy as could be, convinced he
was well on his way to a bright future. Little did he know, the brief bit of
smooth sailing was merely the calm before the storm.

**

The tempest began on Greg's first day back at school after the holidays.
A classmate delivered some terrible news. While Greg was out of town, his
buddy from football camp, Bailey, was killed – an innocent victim of a
drive-by shooting.

Greg was overwhelmed when he heard about what happened.

Make no mistake, it wasn't that he lost a lifelong friend. The two only
knew each other for a few months and only spent a couple days together
during that time. In a sense, though, that was what struck him most. Even
though he considered Bailey a new good friend, he didn't know much about
him at all. They were teenagers with their entire lives ahead of them. Greg
had never felt any sense of urgency to learn much about him.

His dad taught him otherwise when he was little – when Tug died – but
Greg obviously lost sight of that lesson over the years – making it all the
more painful to have to learn again.

A few weeks later, hoping to brighten Greg's spirits, his mom gave him
pictures from their vacation. The annual trip to Hawaii was a highlight of the
year – seven or eight families all staying at the same hotel – and the pictures
did reflect all the fun they had.

But Greg knew the pictures didn't tell the whole story.

Despite being in a location best described as paradise, he complained to
his parents about how "unfair" life is – because he had to share a hotel room
with his sister.

Under any circumstance, he knew he should be embarrassed by the lack of gratitude and maturity he displayed. But now, knowing what happened to Bailey during that same period of time, he was not just embarrassed by his lack of perspective. He was ashamed.

**

For many high school seniors, spring is a time of great anxiety. They complete their K-12 education, and they find out if the universities of their dreams accept them.

For Greg, it was a time of *anticipation*. He applied to some of the nation's most prestigious schools, and he expected to get into all of them.

He could not contain his excitement about the road ahead. His friend, Charlie, was going to the Ivy Leagues. Everyone thought he was brilliant after they heard the news. They called him 'Harvard Charlie'.

Greg felt certain he'd be looked at the same way once he was accepted into the Ivy Leagues, too. He was going to be *one of them*.

Then, one by one, the responses from the schools arrived in Greg's mailbox. They all said the same thing.

No.

In the end, Greg was rejected from every college he wanted to attend. His fast track to success was completely derailed, and he had no idea what went wrong.

He called each school, desperately hoping there had been a mistake. They insisted there was none. He felt like the world was collapsing around him. And yet, things were about to get even worse.

A few months earlier, during the application process, Greg asked a teacher named Avery P. Welton to write a recommendation letter for him. Mr. Welton eventually agreed to do it – but only after first saying he did not want to do it because he did not think Greg applied to schools that were the right 'fit'.

Now that the schools replied – and apparently agreed with Welton's initial opinion – Greg hoped the instructor could help him make sense of it.

Welton told Greg there was no way to know for sure what tipped the scales against him, but he said he did have an idea what might have done it. It was then that Welton gave him a copy of the 'recommendation' letter.

As he read it, Greg went from confused to crushed. The letter did say he was hard-working and succeeded at most everything he tried. That praise, however, was weaved within a web of criticism and ridicule. In the letter of 'recommendation', Welton claimed Greg had poor diction, little charm and asked questions that suggested he had no idea what was going on. He mocked Greg's interest in poetry. He even wrote that Greg, who was being recruited by some of the colleges for sports, had a complete minimum of athletic talent.

The words would've hurt coming from anyone at any time. But to know they were written by someone he thought was in his corner? In a letter that impacted the rest of his life? Greg didn't know whether to scream or cry.

When pressed for an explanation, Welton insisted he did it for the kid's own good. When Greg refused to lower his dreams and went ahead with his plan to apply to Ivy League-level schools, Welton said he took the matter into his own hands – writing a letter of 'recommendation' actually designed to hurt Greg's chances of getting in.

He knew Greg and his family would be upset when they saw the letter, but he insisted he did them a favor in the long run. He claimed that the young man didn't have the brains to cut it at such elite schools.

Greg was devastated.

Charlie said, "It reminded me of when we were little kids and his dog died. He was *that* heartbroken."

Greg's Grandma didn't like seeing her grandson pitying himself.

She huffed, "How many times have I said not to dwell on things that don't go the way you hoped? Some colleges turned you down. Life goes on. Stop feeling sorry for yourself! You gotta get up and keep going."

In the end, as always, Grandma won out.

(8) Never let failure keep you from trying again.

Greg tried to move forward by contacting the universities and urging them to reconsider. When none would reverse their decision, he swallowed his pride and called other schools – some he never even heard of – to beg them to give him a chance. Finally, mercifully, he found a school that would take him. A school located in… *Louisiana???*

**

In the fall, Greg boarded a plane with his bags by his side and a chip on his shoulder. For the record, his anger had nothing to do with Louisiana. He had nothing against the place at all. How could he? He had never been there (or anywhere else in the Deep South, for that matter). In his entire life, he had only met a couple people from the state, and they'd been very kind to him. And, on some level, after the painful embarrassment he felt as a result of Mr. Welton's recommendation letter and the college rejections, part of him was happy to escape to a place so far away.

Still, to be certain, he had no intention of staying in Louisiana for long.

Night after night, he stayed up late and studied. He was determined to get the grades he needed to transfer to one of the Ivy League schools where he was "supposed to go" and get his grand life plan "back on track."

When he wasn't studying for his own classes, he helped kids at a local grade school study for theirs. He saw each kid he tutored – each kid he encouraged to chase a dream – as a chance to turn the negative in his own life into a positive in someone else's life.

At the very least, tutoring was a great distraction. Every minute he spent focused on those kids was a minute not spent dwelling on the detour he was so unhappy that his life took.

Between classes, homework, volunteering and his daily visits to the gym, Greg's schedule quickly filled up. There was only one thing missing.

Friends.

While his classmates got to know each other and enjoyed the freedom college brings, the Ivy League reject viewed himself like a wrongly imprisoned man. He insisted he had been denied the "constitutional right" to attend the college of his choice.

He even went so far as to put up a Martin Luther King, Jr. poster outside his dorm room door, pull his mattress into the hall and stage his own (ridiculous) version of a sit-in.

Then, one day, he met a classmate from Texas named Galloway. She had a point of view unlike any he ever heard. Galloway was accepted to most of the schools to which Greg applied, but she chose Louisiana instead.

"I picked the school that was the best fit for me," she explained.

Greg didn't want to be rude, but this was the craziest thing he ever heard. He felt like he had to say something to her about her decision to turn down the schools attended by the "really smart" kids.

The girl from Texas listened to him politely before responding.

"We had different 'dream schools', but that doesn't mean one of us is wrong. It just means our dreams were different. Stanford, Princeton and those others are great schools, but so is this one. There are really smart kids here, too. And if you open your mind a little and give the place a chance, you might meet them, and you might see why so many of us like it here."

It was a reality check Greg sorely needed. He made more of an effort to meet his classmates and get involved on campus. In the process, he realized Galloway was right. There were a lot of bright students in his classes, and there was a lot to like about the school and Louisiana.

(9) Respect the goals and dreams of others as if they were your own

As it turned out, that conversation was only one of several events over the next few months that made Greg stop and think. His first semester of college also was an election season, and it was no ordinary one. Of the two men trying to become the next governor of Louisiana, one was an alleged racist and anti-Semite. The other had a long history of alleged corruption.

The election brought the issues of race, culture, ethics and power front and center. It would not be the only situation that did.

During that same period, some Native American groups around the country protested against a number of sports teams. They said the teams' names and mascots degraded Native American culture and history. Other people strongly disagreed. They insisted the names and mascots were a 'tribute'. They said the Native American groups were being too politically correct and overly sensitive.

Then, there were the L.A. Riots. A group of white policemen were accused of beating up an unarmed black man. A jury found them not guilty, despite the fact the assault was caught on video. After the jury's decision was announced, riots broke out around Los Angeles. Even before the verdict and its violent aftermath, the videotaped beating and the reaction to it demonstrated that our nation was still a divided one in many ways.

Many black citizens said the incident reinforced their belief they were treated differently by the police. Many white people agreed the attack was horrible, but they insisted it was a very rare exception to the heroic work that most officers around the country do every day.

With all of these events taking place, Greg paid more attention to the racial climate around him. He concluded that there didn't seem to be any tension between students of different backgrounds on his campus. Everybody seemed to get along fine. In many cases, though, he also noticed there didn't seem to be much interaction between them. The groups seemed to be *co-existing side by side* instead of *co-existing together.*

Nowhere was that more clear than it was by The Benches.

In the middle of campus, there were two sets of benches a few feet apart. Every day, dozens if not hundreds of students spent time there in between classes – laughing, joking and socializing with friends.

Over time, Greg noticed a pattern. Every afternoon, almost without fail, the black students hung out by one set of benches. The white students hung out by the other set of benches. Few students ever seemed to cross the invisible line between them.

To be clear, there were no "Whites Only" and "Blacks Only" signs. The separation was voluntary. Still, the situation bothered Greg.

Make no mistake, he did the same thing everyone else seemed to do. Day after day, he visited The Benches and sat with the students who looked like him. And rest assured, he didn't think there was anything wrong with people having friends of the same race. It was simply that he figured everyone's lives would be that much more interesting if they expanded their circle a little. He couldn't understand why nobody, himself included, seemed to take that first step toward bridging the gap between The Benches.

As the days passed, the questions continued to swirl around his head.

How can the choices for Governor come down to a man who appears to be corrupt and another who appears to be racist and anti-Semitic? Why do so many white and black people seem to have different perceptions of police officers? If Native American-related names and mascots are a 'tribute', why aren't there teams called 'Caucasians' or 'Hispanics'? Aren't they worthy of 'tributes', too? Some Native Americans are protesting the teams' names and mascots. Should the teams respect their request to change them? What if other Native Americans take pride in the names and mascots? What should the teams do then? Why do students seem to divide into groups based on race by The Benches? Why doesn't someone bridge the gap between The Benches? What would happen if someone did?

With all of these questions running through his mind, Greg became even more interested in studying issues like diversity and discrimination. He signed up for courses such as Civil Rights, History of Anti-Semitism and Race & Gender. He wrote papers on stereotypes in the media, the use of Native American imagery and names in athletics, and the impact of race in the justice system.

In the process, his own misguided sense of being 'denied a constitutional right' was put back into proper perspective. Obviously, he had not been denied any when his first-choice colleges rejected him. He stopped foolishly seeing his Dr. King poster as a symbol of the tiny personal obstacles he endured en route to college and finally saw the poster for what it was intended to be: A reminder that we all can and should be more than a bystander when we see chances to make a difference in our community.

The more Greg thought about that, the more he wondered what *he* could do to build a bridge between The Benches. What could he do to bring people of different races, cultures and backgrounds together?

It was right then and there, sitting on a mattress in a college dorm in Louisiana, with the poster of Dr. King looking over his shoulder, that a milkshake-drinking, Ivy League reject dreamed up a *Dream* of his own.

It would be years until Greg revealed his *Dream* – or even that he had one. In the meantime, his civic efforts continued to grow. He joined a group on campus for students interested in community service. He also recruited his classmates to volunteer with him at the local grade school where he helped out a couple days a week.

In the summer, he worked for a U.S. Senator in Washington D.C. For Greg, the internship was a powerful introduction to the good side of public service. The Senator was a longtime public servant – serving in the military before coming to Capitol Hill. His staff was inspiring, too. They worked long hours day after day to try and help the citizens back home.

Not surprisingly, Greg's stint in D.C. was also marked by a number of memorable adventures. On one occasion, while attending the Presidential Convention, he was asked to go on stage and check the microphone. Greg did as asked – except that, instead of saying 'Testing 1-2-3', he started to give a pretend speech like he was the person running for office.

A staffer later laughed, "You gotta realize, this took place in the morning before the Convention started. The kid gave his 'speech' to a sound check guy and about 15,000 empty seats."

The summer spent in D.C. motivated Greg to expand his civic efforts when he returned to Louisiana in the fall. In addition to volunteering in the neighborhood, he 'brought the community to campus'. He arranged for the kids he tutored at local schools to sit in his classes, attend college basketball games and meet his professors.

The idea proved popular. Even the Dean volunteered his time to greet the local kids when they came to campus – a defining moment that showed Greg there were people in positions of authority who will respect and support young people who take the initiative to launch a new idea to make a positive difference at their school or in their community.

By the end of his sophomore year, Greg had come a long way.

Academically, he excelled. He had an A in every single course. His efforts to encourage others to volunteer led the Dean to appoint him Chairman of Community Service for the whole college. Socially, considering his rocky start, he came far, too. His classmates elected him to class office. He even joined a fraternity.

Some people were surprised by the latter. The backpack-toting, civic-minded member of Student Government didn't exactly fit the stereotypical image of a Frat Boy. But, in reality, at least in this case, that's all that image was. A stereotype. Yes, the fraternity threw parties, but its members studied a lot and volunteered a lot, too. The fraternity did play host to some late nights, but it also was a place where valuable lessons were learned.

Of all the ones Greg learned, the one he probably needed most was taught to him by a guy called Red Juice (RJ, for short).

Nicknamed for his cranberry-colored hair, RJ was one of the funniest people Greg ever met. At least, that's what he thought until he realized that RJ's one-liners always seemed to be about *him*. Still as sensitive as ever, Greg angrily demanded RJ stop making fun of him.

"You gotta lighten up," the easy-going Southerner laughed. "I'm not making fun of you. I'm just cracking jokes."

Greg said he didn't understand the difference.

RJ replied, "Nobody else is here but us when I do it."

It was true. In front of others, RJ spoke well of his friends. He only told the jokes when they were alone.

**

Two years after landing in Louisiana, Greg sincerely enjoyed life in the Deep South. But there was still one thing missing. Something that always lingered in the back of his mind. For all the things Louisiana was, there was one thing it wasn't and never would be.

The Ivy Leagues.

No matter how much Greg liked Louisiana, he still wished for a chance to prove he could succeed at the schools that rejected him. He decided to stick to his original plan and transfer in the fall.

The Dean insisted he was making a huge mistake. He said that Greg was doing very well in Louisiana and should think twice before giving it all up for the chance to start over at some other school.

"It's not some other school," Greg insisted. "It's the Ivy Leagues."

The Dean held firm, reminding him that the grass isn't always greener on the other side. His advice fell on deaf ears. Greg's mind was made. It seemed like nothing was going to change it.

Then, the Dean told him about Junior Year Abroad – the program that lets college students spend time studying in another country.

Other than a short trip to the Middle East when he was a boy, Greg never crossed the ocean. He was intrigued by the idea of going overseas.

"What do the students study when they're in the program?" he asked.

The Dean explained that was the best part of all. Depending on where a student chose to go, there was a wide range of subjects he or she could study – from how to speak another language to how to make movies.

Greg already learned another language (Spanish), but the moment he heard those four magic words – how to make movies – he lit up like a Christmas tree. The thought of reaching Goal #1 from *The First Thirty* – winning an Academy Award ® for his first film – danced around his head. Quicker than you can say *popcorn*, Greg scrapped the plan that seemed so set in stone a few moments earlier. Instead of seeking an Ivy League transfer, he'd spend his junior year in Europe learning about filmmaking and then come back to Louisiana to wrap up college and get his degree.

When summer arrived, Greg went home with a sense of excitement about the road ahead and the voyage to Europe in the fall. With time on his hands until the trip, however, his mind began to wander. Was the trip abroad really about learning to make films? Or was it an excuse to avoid transferring and finding out if he could succeed in the Ivy Leagues? By the time summer wound down, second thoughts crept into his head.

His mother urged him to focus his energy on the future instead of thinking about what might have been.

Her words made sense, but in the heat of the moment, they upset her sensitive son.

He stormed out of the house and went for a drive to calm down. He intended to go see his Grandma, but he was too frustrated to think clearly about directions. A wrong turn there. A u-turn here. Before long, he got lost.

While trying to get back on the right route, Greg unexpectedly drove by the campus of Vernon Froehmann Whitfield University.

Since it was not on the East Coast, VFWU was not part of the Ivy Leagues, but it might as well have been. By all accounts, it was one of the most highly regarded universities in the nation.

Greg sat in his car and watched the students pass by him. They wore shirts and shorts and hats bearing the school's name and colors. They all looked so happy.

He became consumed with jealousy. He knew the students walking down the sidewalk were all probably much brighter than he was, but he refused to believe they were *better*. In his heart, Greg knew he would've outworked them all if only he'd been given the chance.

Now that he was this close, he had to know, if only for a few seconds, what it was like to be *one of them*.

He got out of his car and slipped into the crowd of students. He only meant to walk a few feet. With each step forward, though, it became harder to stick to that plan. With each step, he became more convinced he fit in. He became more convinced that he *was* one of them. And once and for all, he decided, he was going to prove it.

His heart racing, his confidence soaring, he veered off the sidewalk, into a school office and declared he was there to enroll.

When he got home a few hours later, his mom was in the kitchen. When he walked in, she asked, "Where have you been all day?"

"Vernon Froehmann Whitfield University," he said.

"Visiting friends?" she asked.

"No," he said, with tears in his eyes. "I go there now."

(10) No matter the odds against you,
they almost always improve if you show up

As impossible as it may seem, Greg had shown up unannounced at one of the nation's top universities, decided on the spot he wanted to go there and talked his way in.

Well, sort of.

In fact, he struck something of a deal. He could attend classes for one year like the 'real' students. He would receive grades in those classes like the 'real' students. If he did well, he could stay. If he didn't do well, he had to leave – and there would be no refund.

For the school, there was nothing to lose. For Greg, his entire future was at risk. But it was a gamble he felt he had to take. He wanted to prove he never should have been rejected from all those schools three years earlier. He wanted to prove Mr. Welton was wrong. He wanted to prove to everyone back home that he could keep up with the 'really smart' kids. He wanted to prove he was good enough to be *one of them*.

Vernon Froehmann Whitfield University seemed to have everything a student could want. There were brilliant professors, interesting courses, talented classmates and a beautiful campus.

But for Greg, the opportunity to go there came at a very steep price.

As his old Dean warned, he was now like a freshman starting from scratch. Finding his way to class was a challenge. The assignments piled up on his lap. In every sense of the word, he felt *overwhelmed*.

Things soon went from bad to worse.

Within days of setting foot on campus, Greg clashed with some of the people in charge at Froehmann Whitfield.

Shortly after he signed up for his classes, he requested a meeting with a school official. He was told he needed to wait his turn.

"The lady told me to make an appointment," he muttered angrily. "They don't consider me a real student. They'd never say that to a real student!"

In fairness to the official, he wasn't one of the real students, and she did say that to the real ones, too. To an impartial observer, that was obvious. It was unreasonable for Greg to expect someone overseeing thousands of students to meet with him at the drop of a hat. He was simply wrong. In his defense, though, that level of access was all he had ever known.

Mortimer Dowhill was a small high school with an 'open door policy' that gave students the chance to talk directly with administrators with little else required besides a knock when they entered. Louisiana was bigger, but Greg served in several student leadership positions. As a result, the Dean and other school officials always made time for him.

The new student in town didn't fare too well off campus, either.

Greg got a job delivering food on weekends, but he kept getting lost. He only managed to make three deliveries during his first shift and was fired.

The manager shrugged, "You're a nice guy, but I can't have you deliver food if you can't find the places where you're supposed to deliver it."

The manager was right, of course. But that did not matter to Greg. Those old feelings – that nobody believed in his abilities – resurfaced. The chip on his shoulder grew bigger and bigger by the day. Instead of putting up the poster of Dr. King in his new apartment, he put up a poster of a snarling dog.

He was angry, lonely and overwhelmed, but he refused to quit. As in Louisiana, he used some of his free time to volunteer. It was a productive way to distract himself from thinking about the things that upset him. In this case, he tutored former gang members trying to get their high school degree. He also worked out his frustration through daily visits to the gym.

Of course, nothing put him in a better mood than spending time with his Grandma. Now that he was attending college ten minutes down the road from her apartment, he was able to see her in person on a more regular basis – cementing the bond that was already the strongest one he had.

Exercising, volunteering and visiting his Grandma. That was it. Other than an occasional date, virtually every other minute was spent in class or studying for one. He woke up early and stayed up late. He spent whatever time was necessary to do his homework and prepare for his courses.

In the end, that tunnel vision paid off. Despite the odds against someone showing up out of nowhere, adjusting to a new environment and acing his classes, that's what Greg did. During his year at VFWU, he received an A in every course.

Ironically, even after proving he belonged and earning the right to formally transfer into the school, he maintained a certain distance from his peers. Some of them went out of their way to try and include him in their plans, but he rarely accepted. When other students went to eat, he stayed home to study. When they went to parties or basketball games, he studied.

It was as if he was still more interested in *proving* he should be one of them than actually *being* one of them.

To add to his troubles, Greg continued to argue with school officials.

Charlie recalled, "There were a whole list of things they did that upset him. He called me at least once a week with the latest. The one that comes to mind first was the thing with his credits."

In many cases, when a student switches colleges, he or she has to stay an extra semester or two and take a couple extra classes because the new school has different requirements for graduation than the first one. It was perfectly routine, but when it happened to Greg, he was convinced he was being singled out.

"They're questioning my qualifications!" he barked. "It's not fair!"

He fired off angry letters demanding administrators leave him alone.

He spent an increasing amount of time in the weight room to work out his frustration. Before long, the results started to show. By the time his final year of college rolled around, the skinny boy afraid of the neighbor's dog had transformed into a young man bench-pressing 300 pounds.

A friend and college neighbor named Kim laughed, "He stood in the mirror and flexed over and over. It wasn't in a look-how-tough-I-am kind of way. It was more of an I-was-skinnier-than-a-toothpick-where-did-these-muscles-come-from kind of way. It was funny to see the expression on his face. I'd never seen him so happy."

His joy was short-lived.

"Nobody changes that much," cynics howled. "You took steroids!"

The comments were dumb. It may have seemed like his body changed overnight, but there was nothing sudden about it. He had lifted weights for years now, drank those weight-gain shakes for even longer, finally ate more food, and he had genetics on his side. His father, Mark, was six foot three and over two hundred pounds.

Greg was deeply hurt by the remarks, but Grandma had little patience for his whining.

She huffed, "Why do you care what those people say? *You* know what you did and what you didn't. That's the only thing that matters."

As always, her tough love helped. He resumed his workouts and did his best to ignore those who questioned him.

Greg's progress in the weight room was outmatched only by his success in the classroom. Five years after being told he wasn't good enough for the Ivy Leagues, and three years after walking into Vernon Froehmann Whitfield University right off the street, he graduated with Highest Distinction. In all, he finished college with 37 A's and a B.

He had every right to be proud of what he accomplished. Despite all the detours and obstacles, he kept chugging along until he achieved his dream – a sterling transcript at a school with a reputation that he was certain would impress his parents, Mr. Welton, Charlie and everyone else back home.

Yet, at what should have been a crowning moment, all Greg felt was regret. For all the great things VFWU was, there was one thing missing. One thing it wasn't and never would be.

Louisiana.

Greg missed his professors and the Dean. He missed the local kids he tutored. He missed his friends and fraternity brothers. He missed the weather, the culture, the music and the Southern hospitality.

Having been at VFWU for three years, he understood why so many students thought it was a great place and wanted to attend the school.

But he went there for the wrong reason.

And he knew it.

Ever since the 'recommendation letter' nightmare, he insisted a 'measly piece of paper' could not define who he was or what he could achieve. Yet, he gave up what he loved in Louisiana – not to mention, the chance to study film in Europe – all for the chance to get a diploma with a name on it that he thought would make a greater impression on people back home.

The kid who insisted he should not be measured by a piece of paper sacrificed everything for… a piece of paper.

And now, instead of symbolizing the success he achieved at VFWU, that piece of paper served only as a painful reminder of what he gave up to be there.

He felt so strongly about it that he said he never wanted to see his diploma a single time. He even decided to skip the graduation ceremony where the degrees were handed out.

His Grandma was furious. She said a graduate skipping the graduation ceremony was like a runner not crossing the finish line in a marathon.

"And what about me?" she growled. "I've got pictures of all my other grandkids in their caps and gowns. You have to go to that ceremony. Otherwise, I won't have a picture of you graduating college!"

Despite how strongly she felt, Greg defied her orders.

He skipped the ceremony.

In fact, he never even picked up his diploma.

To try to patch things up with his disappointed Grandma, Greg promised her that somehow, some day, he would bring her a picture of him 'crossing another stage' in a cap and gown.

**

As one of VFWU's top graduates, Greg appeared to have a bright and profitable future. If, that is, he followed the 'regular' path.

Despite his degree and the honors that came with it, he didn't want to interview for any lucrative corporate jobs. He didn't want to apply to grad school, either. He agreed those were great options for some people, but they were not the right ones for him. At least, not now.

He explained to his parents that his up-and-down road caused him to reconsider his future. When choosing a career path, he now believed the most important thing was *finding his fit.*

Instead of considering factors like *What will make me money?*, he began to ask himself questions like *What will make me happy?*

"And that," he explained to his parents, "is why I've decided to set all my old goals on hold and spend one year as a teacher."

Mark and Rose were stunned. They knew their son enjoyed the time he spent volunteering at local schools while he was in college, but they never dreamed he would pursue a career as an educator. Make no mistake, they thought teaching was a fine profession – just not for Greg. He had not taken a single class in the field of teaching while in college. And besides, with his grades, there was a pot of gold waiting for him in corporate America.

Hoping some time in the sun could bring his oldest child to his senses (or, at least, distract him), Mark gave Greg a ticket to California as his graduation gift.

The plan almost worked. The chance to be near Hollywood caused him to think once again about pursuing his dream to write books and films, but he still couldn't get teaching out of his head.

He packed his bags and headed home.

"Maybe, one day, I'll go back to California," Greg told his mom and dad. "Maybe, one day, I'll go to law school or business school. Maybe, one day, I'll join corporate America. But none of those one day's are today. Today, I've gotta follow my heart. And my heart is telling me to teach."

Since he did not have the proper credentials to be a full-time teacher, he signed up to be a substitute.

He knew 'substitute teacher' was a far cry from the path most kids in his position choose to follow. It certainly wasn't going to bring a salary like the one Charlie received from the global consulting firm that hired him after graduation. Still, he was certain. This was the direction he wanted to go. He wanted to spend one year working with kids, and he wanted to do it now – in case there never was a chance to do it later.

**

In preparation for his new job, Greg moved into a one bedroom apartment in a high-rise building in the city. Its window happened to overlook The Green – the neighborhood where he expected to do most of his work as a substitute teacher.

While he waited for the call to get started, Greg put the extra free time to use by trying yet again to learn the skill that eluded him all his life – how to draw. This time, he decided to teach himself.

Charlie laughed loudly when he heard the idea.

"How can you teach yourself something you don't know?"

Charlie did seem to have a point, but Greg didn't care. He sat down and drew some new pictures. Not surprisingly, the new sketches were as bad as the ones he drew when he was little. But he loved art. So, he stuck with it. He spent hours and hours on each drawing, trying to learn from his mistakes along the way.

Somehow, over time, the sketches started to improve. They still weren't very good, but they were good enough to motivate Greg to keep working at it on a nightly basis.

To fill the rest of his time, he helped his dad with finance work during the week and lifted weights at the gym in the evenings. For weekends, he lined up a job working at a new restaurant/bar called The Club.

The Club was a classy, upscale place that quickly became *the place to be* for top executives (and had a line down the street to prove it).

Greg's job was an easy one. He stood by the door, greeted customers and checked the bathroom once an hour to make sure it was clean.

As usual, though, there were bumps in the road.

He was fired after one night.

It was the result of a misunderstanding. The Boss thought Greg took ten dollars he wasn't supposed to take. But it hardly seemed to be worth fighting over. The job only paid a few bucks an hour. He only held the job for one night. He could easily get a similar job at another restaurant. Besides, he planned to quit in a couple months once he began his stint as a substitute teacher. The logical thing was to walk away, but Greg refused to do it until he wrote a note to The Boss to protest his innocence and clear things up.

Within hours of getting the note, The Boss realized a mistake probably had been made, called to apologize and even offered to re-hire him.

Greg was stunned by the call and the humility of The Boss. He knew this was someone he could learn from. So much so, he accepted the offer to return to his job as part-time doorman and even decided to keep working there on weekends after he started substitute teaching.

(11) If you come across someone you can learn from,
make the effort to be around them as much as you can

On his first day as a sub, Greg was assigned to Blue Academy. The school was located in The Green – that neighborhood he could see a few blocks away from the window in his high-rise apartment.

He never stepped foot in The Green before his first day on the job as a teacher, but he certainly heard stories about it. Everybody had. Stories about drugs and violence and despair. He also heard white people were not too welcome there.

At one point, those myths might have been enough to scare him away. Now, he knew to keep an open mind. After the big guys in the weight room and his classmates in Louisiana both showed him how wrong assumptions can be, he knew not to pre-judge a place where he had never been.

And so it was, on a cold January morning, a twenty-four year old part-time restaurant doorman strolled out his door, past the train tracks and into The Green for his first day as a substitute teacher.

As it turned out, Greg did have problems that first day, but it had nothing to do with the neighborhood. It had to do with teaching.

He didn't know how.

That first day, after being greeted graciously by Principal Brooks and his warm-hearted clerk, Ms. Boggs, inside Blue Academy's front door, Greg was given a room number and sent on his way. He assumed it was the room where he would be trained. But when he walked in, he discovered it was an actual class with actual students expecting him to teach them something.

The kids behaved fine, but Greg quickly found himself overwhelmed. The day was a complete disaster. In the weeks that followed, the job didn't get much easier. He found out the hard way that knowing something and being able to teach it were two different things (especially while monitoring twenty or twenty-five students at once).

The experience frustrated Greg to no end. The veteran, full-time teachers made it look so effortless – like jugglers gracefully tossing six bowling pins at once. When he tried to do it, the pins all fell to the ground.

Night after night, Greg stayed awake, staring out the window, wishing he could be as effective as the full-time teachers. Until finally, one time, tired of his sleepless nights, he – literally – threw out his bed.

It would be seven long months until he got a new one.

On the bright side, there was one thing Greg did do well – names. He memorized a class full of them in minutes. The kids were amazed he could do it. More than anything, they wondered why he bothered. After all, he was a sub. It's not like he would be in the class every day for the rest of the year.

He always responded the same way. He told them that whether he was there for one day or forever, he still wanted to know them as individuals instead of assuming they were all the same.

"And the first step in doing that," he told them, "is knowing your names. Names set us apart from each other. Names remind us that each of us is a human being. Not a statistic or a number."

It was an explanation he repeated so often that one kid drew a cartoon of him saying it. Years later, another student sent him a note thanking him for the difference he made in her life. Her note ended with a memorable line: "Thank you again for knowing my name."

(12) Never underestimate the value of knowing someone's name.
A person's name is the most important word in the world.

As he got to know the students better, Greg found the biggest obstacle for some of them had little to do with confidence in themselves. It had to do with confidence in others. Having seen some people in their community treated poorly because of where they live or the color of their skin, some of the kids questioned whether they would get a fair shake to succeed when they got older – even if they did put in the necessary time and effort.

Searching for a way to convince them they could accomplish anything – even if they had to create their own opportunity to do it – Greg told the kids about his lifelong struggle with art and his current efforts to teach himself how to draw. Then, he pulled out the scrapbook where he kept his sketches. This gave the students the chance to see his progress with their own eyes.

A twenty-four year old rookie educator, twenty-five kids and a book of drawings. Little did anyone know that moment in time set off a ripple effect that changed Greg's life – and thousands of others – for years to come.

**

It was a cool weekend morning when Greg walked out his door to pick up his sister for brunch. At the same time, two boys from Blue Academy happened to be heading down the same street on their way to get sodas.

The moment they saw Greg, they recognized him as a result of his art (they didn't even remember his name – only that he was the new substitute teacher who could draw) and hustled ahead to say hello.

After talking to the kids for a bit and learning they were on their way to get sodas, Greg offered to get them milkshakes if they wanted to join him and his sister instead. The two boys quickly accepted.

The three walked and talked as they made their way toward the building where Greg's sister lived a few blocks away. When they arrived, they found out she had changed her mind. She was upset that her brother got distracted on the way to get her and was late to pick her up.

"I guess it's just the three of us," Greg said with a shrug.

They walked another few blocks before arriving at Gordon Birchwood's Terrace. It was a popular, casual restaurant located in an affluent part of town. It was the first time Greg or the boys ever went there for a meal.

When they arrived, the hostess greeted them with a warm welcome and seated them at a table next to two white women. As the trio sat down, one of the ladies gave the two African-American boys a look of disdain and moved her purse to the far side of her table in a way that suggested she was afraid one of them might steal it.

Greg was enraged. How could she make a presumption about two kids she never met? As far as he was concerned, it made no sense.

A series of questions rapidly swirled around his head.

Was it his place to do something about what he witnessed? This didn't happen in a classroom where he was the teacher and authority figure. It happened at a restaurant where he was just a customer... If it was his place to intervene, what could he actually do? He was a 24-year-old substitute teacher who worked as a doorman on weekends. He was not powerful or rich... It was a brief incident in which no punches – or even any words – were exchanged. Was it a 'big enough' moment to require a response at all?

The answers came to him quickly. Based on what he experienced and learned while he was a student, he believed we all have a civic responsibility to make our community a welcoming place. He knew a young person can make a meaningful impact if they stay committed and positive. And he knew that if intolerance is not addressed during the seemingly 'small' moments, history tells us that there is a risk it will lead to bigger ones.

He rose from his seat, approached the head of the restaurant and said, "Do you see those two kids? I'm coming back with ten."

At first, Greg's plan was to return with ten African-American students to prove a point to the woman with the purse.

But a short time later, he reconsidered his approach.

He explained, "I realized the lady with the purse probably wouldn't even be at the restaurant when we returned a week or two later. Instead of worrying about her, I decided to focus my response on us – to bring people of different ages and backgrounds together around one table so they can get to know each other over a meal."

Initially, as people heard about the incident, most presumed the woman was driven by racial stereotypes. In later years, as that 'milkshake moment' became the subject of countless discussions in the press and in classrooms, some observers were not quite as quick to jump to that conclusion. Maybe, they said, her reaction had less to do with disliking African-American kids in particular and more to do with disliking kids in general. After all, she didn't *say* anything. How can anyone be *certain* her actions were based on the kids' race? There *are* older adults who don't like to be around *any* kids.

It was a valid point – an important one, even – making it that much more significant that Greg chose to respond the way he did.

A teacher observed, "History tells us that, more likely than not, the students' race was a factor in that customer's decision to do what she did, but given that Greg knew nothing about her and she did not say anything, we cannot know for sure. The valuable lesson is how Greg responded. Instead of him making assumptions about the person who appeared to make assumptions about the two kids, and then letting that determine his response, he shifted the focus to a positive new initiative."

(13) People don't remember how you are treated.
They remember how you respond.

Greg was eager to pursue his plan, but reality settled in a short time later. Before the return visit to Birchwood's Terrace could take place, he needed to find students who wanted to go, get their parents' permission and come up with a way to pay for the whole thing.

He enthusiastically made calls all over the city. Within ten days, he rounded up seven kids and a parent to come with him back to Birchwood's, but he still had no idea how to pay for the group meal.

With two days to go, as he headed over to The Club for another night on the job as a doorman, he decided he had only one remaining option (other than paying the whole bill himself) – talk to one of The Club's wealthy clients and ask them to foot the bill.

Greg knew the chance that a customer granted that kind of request from a doorman was slim. He also knew he could lose his job for asking. Still, he felt it was a risk he had to take.

Luckily, it paid off.

The first customer Greg approached was the CEO of a local company.

After hearing what the young doorman wanted to do and why, The CEO agreed to pay for the brunch. He even agreed to personally attend.

That Sunday, Greg returned to Birchwood's Terrace like he vowed to do. The ten people who came with him ended up being the seven kids and one parent, plus The CEO and one of The CEO's friends.

The brunch was everything Greg hoped for and more. The food and milkshakes were delicious, the staff treated them wonderfully, and everyone at the table had a great time.

It was likely at that moment – sipping a shake, surrounded by a diverse group of people all getting along – that Greg knew he stumbled onto the world he wanted to be part of. A world where people co-existed *together* instead of merely co-existing *side by side.*

He also knew he didn't want to see it end as quickly as it started.

A week turned into a month. Greg was still returning to that same restaurant every Sunday. Each week, he brought five to ten of his friends – adults from every walk of life – and an equal number of students. The adults each paid for themselves and one kid. The students each paid a dollar to remind them "nothing in life is free."

In many ways, Greg was following the blueprint he mapped out in Louisiana – giving kids a chance to meet people who could mentor them about college and careers – but there was one big difference. This time, he also focused on giving kids a chance to meet and learn from each other.

To achieve that goal, he went out of his way to invite students from all different backgrounds to attend the brunches.

Some people questioned the value of including so-called *rich kids*, but Greg insisted on it. He knew the only way to get kids from different backgrounds past the stereotypes they hear and read about each other was to bring them all together and give them the chance to meet face-to-face.

The adults came from all different backgrounds, too.

There was no official 'theme' at any particular brunch. Greg wanted the participants to talk about the same things they usually discussed over a meal – college, careers, music, sports, fashion, politics. What made it special was they were discussing these topics with people outside of their regular circle of friends. As a result, they could hear a fresh set of opinions.

With a focus on the value of different perspectives, Greg wanted all of them – the kids and adults – to approach the brunches like they had something to learn and something to teach.

One adult named Cresta said, "That concept is what drew me to the table. We didn't wear ID tags that said *Volunteers* and *Students*. We were all just *People*. It was an environment based on mutual respect, where everyone treated every other person at the table as a potential source of wisdom. The kids could learn from us, but we realized we could learn from them, too."

In the process of bringing these diverse people together, Greg created a full-fledged program. He even gave the group a name.

The Brunch Bunch.

It wasn't too fancy-sounding, but neither was the group. They were a bunch of people going to brunch. Nothing more, nothing less.

Until, that is, Mr. Landers heard about them. Mr. Landers, whose company runs health clubs, appreciated what Greg was trying to do. One of his health clubs happened to be a few blocks from the restaurant. So, Mr. Landers offered to let the group come play basketball after brunch.

After seeing how well the kids behaved, he said Greg could bring them back for an hour every week.

As one kid said, "Milkshakes and b-ball, it doesn't get much better."

The Brunch Bunch suddenly had a routine. They ate at Birchwood's. Then, they went down the street to play basketball for an hour. To wrap up the day, the kids wrote thank you notes to the adults who attended the lunch and the staff members at the restaurant and the health club.

**

Birchwood's Terrace was not the only restaurant Greg visited every week. Every Tuesday, he stopped by the same place to get lunch. He always ordered the same thing: turkey and lettuce on a bagel.

One week, as he picked up his order, Greg asked the Manager if there were any leftover bagels.

"If there are," he explained, "I'll give them to the kids at school."

A week later, she gave him three bags full of them.

The kids loved the bagels, and the Manager loved helping the community. Each week, she gave Greg more bagels to pass out at school. Until, one time, she gave him more bagels than there were students.

After school ended that day, he walked around the neighborhood looking for a place to bring the extra bagels. In doing so, he came across a local center for seniors.

The residents at The Center already had food and didn't need the bagels. Nevertheless, they did seem to enjoy the company of an unexpected visitor, and the feeling was clearly mutual.

Despite his already exhausting schedule, Greg made time to visit The Center every Saturday afternoon.

Given the residents' physical condition, he initially talked softly around them. He soon discovered the error of his ways. Wheelchair-bound or not, the seniors were young at heart. They wanted to argue about politics, hear jokes and cheer on their favorite teams. More than anything, they enjoyed telling stories. They didn't merely know history. They had lived it. And they loved to share it.

The more Greg got to know the residents, the more he liked them. They were respectful and worthy of respect. Above all else, they were kind.

One time, he mentioned his Grandma was under the weather. On his next visit, a resident gave him a bag with seven get-well cards – "so you can send one to your Grandma every day of the week."

Before long, as he did in Louisiana, Greg asked his friends to volunteer with him. Many were happy to do it.

Some were less eager – not interested in spending their free time with "old people" – but he stayed on their case until they went at least one time.

Once they did, it usually didn't take long for them to realize why Greg liked it there so much. By the time the hour was up, most of his friends asked if and when they could return and visit the seniors again.

(14) Assumptions and stereotypes work in all directions.
Anyone of any age from any background can be subjected to them unfairly.

In June, Greg's brief stint as a substitute teacher was scheduled to end. For weeks, he mapped out his final day. Instead of teaching that day, he planned to make stops at all the schools where he worked as a substitute throughout the year. He convinced his mom to join him so she could see that his time as an educator had been well spent.

It seemed a fitting end, but the day turned out to be a wreck – capped off by an argument between Rose and an official at one of the schools.

To Greg, it was the same old story. After all his hard work, right when he was about to celebrate his success, something went wrong.

He knew he should put the day out of his mind and move on to the lucrative career in business that awaited him, but he couldn't stand the thought of ending his teaching stint on such a sour note. With the same prove-'em-wrong impulsiveness that caused him to transfer to VFWU instead of studying film in Europe, he decided to take yet another detour.

"I'm going back to substitute teach in the fall," Greg declared.

"Are you serious?" his girlfriend at the time, Sloane, asked.

"A thousand percent serious."

He sounded certain, but he knew it'd be easier said than done.

Months earlier, he promised his parents that he would interview for a corporate job after the year was up. There seemed to be no way out. Until, that is, he came up with the loophole of all loopholes.

Technically speaking, he promised to *interview* for a job that met his parents' approval. He never promised to actually *get* one.

Over the next few weeks, he went on job interviews as promised. But he purposely messed them up. In one interview, he jumped an imaginary rope in the man's office. In another instance, Greg brought a bag of bagels to the meeting – and juggled them. On a third occasion, when asked for a reference, he put down the name of a fourteen year old.

In between purposely ruining interviews, Greg continued to help his students – and continued to learn from them as well.

In one instance, Greg, his girlfriend at the time (Sloane) and his old pal (Charlie) took some kids to their first pro baseball game. One boy, Elliott, wanted to bring his glove so he could catch a foul ball, but Greg told him to forget it – noting that he was more likely to lose the glove than catch a ball.

Elliott refused to give up on his idea. He kept referring to it as "the" foul ball, as if already guaranteed that one would be hit in his direction. Not wanting to be late, Greg finally granted the boy's wish.

Sure enough, in the 7th inning, as 20,000 other fans watched on, Elliott reached his glove up into the air and caught his foul ball.

(15) If you have an idea you believe in, hold your ground, be prepared, and when the moment does arrive, reach up and grab it.

In the fall, having successfully ruined every interview he went on, Greg dusted off his substitute teacher badge and returned to the classroom. His first day back in The Green was certainly a memorable one.

During third period, a drunk man ventured into the school parking lot, climbed on top of the first car (which happened to be Greg's), and hit it repeatedly with a brick. Greg dashed outside, but he was too late. The man already ran off – leaving only the brick in his wake.

A guy sitting across the street encouraged Greg to keep the brick. This way, nobody else picked it up and damaged other cars with it.

Even though the man meant well, the advice did not seem to make much sense. The Green was rapidly changing. The housing projects were being replaced by a community of upscale townhomes. As a result of the ongoing construction, there were hundreds of stray bricks throughout the area. Taking one brick off the street hardly seemed to make much difference.

"What good is one brick?" Greg asked.

The man's response helped inspire another life lesson:

(16) One brick might not be much, but it's one brick better than none.

The situation with the car was unfortunate, but it was an exception. Despite all the supposed dangers lurking in The Green, Greg rarely had a problem there. In fact, most residents made him feel at home.

But that's not to say everyone everywhere appreciated his efforts.

From time to time, when he said he was a substitute teacher, at a dinner party back in his hometown for instance, there were people who asked if he was going to become a *real* teacher at some point.

The question made Greg wince.

He knew substitute teachers weren't *full-time* teachers. He was the first to admit he wasn't a *great* teacher. But being told he wasn't a *real* teacher hit a sore spot for someone who spent much of his life being told he didn't understand the difference between fiction and reality.

The school bell rang around three o'clock, but Greg's days usually lasted much longer. Most nights, he worked out at the gym and then spent an hour or two on the phone putting together that weekend's brunch. (The brunch usually took place on Sunday, but it occasionally took place on Saturday instead. This made it possible for kids who attended religious services every Sunday to still participate.)

The program took up more of Greg's time than he ever dreamed it would, but there was no turning back now. The Brunch Bunch had become part of people's lives. Kids became friends with other kids they would have otherwise never met. They met different adults and learned about different careers. A few of the kids even got offers to work part-time or during the holidays from the adults they impressed at brunch.

And speaking of the adults, so many of them were now offering to volunteer that the program had a waiting list.

Make no mistake, The Brunch Bunch did not magically erase the barriers that have divided society for centuries. From time to time, even at their own table, there were moments of awkward silence and people who felt uncomfortable sitting next to neighbors from such different backgrounds. But the overwhelming majority of people who took part in the program got beyond those hang-ups, got to know the other people at the table and realized their similarities far outweighed their differences.

Upon reaching the group's first anniversary, Greg brought them to other locations around the city. To his delight, the restaurant community embraced the program. Some restaurants even offered to waive the entire bill.

The Brunch Bunch Tour was off and running.

In the weeks that followed, Greg developed some great relationships with the management and staff at the restaurants participating in the brunch program. They appreciated his passion for using their food and beverages as common ground to build bridges within a community.

In turn, the interaction reinforced Greg's appreciation for the men and women in the restaurant and hospitality industry. Day in and day out, they worked hard to serve so many people. He looked forward to being in their presence every weekend.

Some observers questioned whether the guests of the restaurants – especially the upscale locations – would be receptive when "The Bunch" walked through the doors for the first time.

Those doubts proved to be wildly off-base.

Yes, there was an occasional glare or a whisper that reminded Greg of the woman who moved her purse, but those instances were few and far between. Almost always, the customers at these other restaurants were extremely kind and courteous. In one or two cases, they approached the manager and anonymously paid the entire bill for the mentoring program. Every so often, they even approached the table to introduce themselves and ask if they could participate in a future outing.

The latter gesture in particular meant the world to Greg. Those customers had taken the initiative to cross that imaginary yet powerful boundary that keeps people eating at separate tables, co-existing side-by-side instead of co-existing together.

During this same period, Greg continued to volunteer with seniors at The Center every week. After a few months, he was given an unofficial role – Bingo Caller. It was a seemingly straightforward role. For one hour every week, he sat at the head of the table and shouted out the numbers.

Until, one afternoon, he got banned from the game.

"How did you mess up calling Bingo numbers?" Charlie asked.

"I like the residents so much that I couldn't stand to see any of them lose. So, I purposely called out numbers that ensured each of them got a chance to win. I guess, eventually, someone caught on to what I was doing."

He meant well, and the folks at The Center knew it. So, they said he could still visit and help each week. Just no more calling Bingo numbers.

Greg's good intentions nearly cost him his job at The Club, too.

He enjoyed working there. After several months, though, he was anxious to prove he could do more than stand by a door and clean a bathroom. Without being asked, he took on more responsibilities. Seating guests. Serving bread. Clearing dishes.

He thought he was doing a great job.

When The Boss asked to talk with him about all the tasks he was doing without being asked, he figured he was on the verge of getting a promotion or a raise. As it turned out, he almost got fired.

"I know you mean well," The Boss said, "but you're so busy trying to help everyone else that you forget about doing your own job."

Greg replied, "All I basically do is stand there and hold a door and say 'hello' to people who are arriving and 'goodbye' to people who are leaving. Aren't I doing a better job by running around and helping everyone?"

The Boss smiled and said, "Not when I pay you to stand in one place."

(17) A wheel is of no value to a car unless it is spinning in circles.

Greg quietly went back to doing the job he was hired to do.

Not that he really minded.

As the doorman at The Club, he had a unique chance to observe the customers. They were some of the city's most powerful business executives. For hours on end, he stood by that door, studied these people and tried to figure out what made them so successful.

In the process, he also saw what *not* to do.

More than once, for example, he saw wealthy customers talking to a busboy or parking attendant like they were parents scolding a small child.

Even when the customers meant well, some gave into stereotypes. One time, for example, a lady urged Greg to keep working hard and save his money for college tuition (assuming incorrectly that he must not have a degree if he worked as a doorman).

> *(18) The only thing you should assume about a person*
> *based on their job...is that they have one*

In June, Greg's second year as a substitute came to an end. He went on another series of job interviews. This time, he actually wanted to get hired. He still planned to volunteer on the weekends, but Charlie and the others from back home were now well on their way climbing the corporate ladder. Greg was anxious to catch up.

It turned out there was one small problem with his plan.

Nobody wanted to hire him.

A year out of school, Greg was no longer seen as a student who recently graduated with Highest Distinction from a highly regarded university. To most interviewers, his college record was a distant memory. They now saw him strictly as a 'substitute teaching restaurant doorman' – and most of them didn't seem to have much use for one of those. Others felt he was too concerned with civic service to focus on a corporate job. In the end, for one reason or another, he was not offered a single full-time position.

With his own personal dreams slipping away, Greg did what he always did – distracted himself from thinking about it by helping other people. He continued volunteering at The Center every Saturday. The brunch program kept meeting on weekends – 70 straight weeks and counting. He even arranged for a company to donate the money and time needed to build an entire garden inside the empty atrium of a grade school in The Green.

Greg was proud of his efforts, but as long as he was focusing on helping other people, he wished he could do it on a grander scale. And that's when Charlie told him that there was a way that he could. All he had to do was set up something called a NonProfit organization.

As it was explained to Greg, a *For-Profit* company is one which sells products or services in an effort to make money, like a company that sells shoes. A *NonProfit* organization is focused on providing a service to society like helping those in need. A lot of people and companies who are in a position to donate money will *only* donate money to groups that are officially recognized as NonProfit companies.

Greg had no experience running a NonProfit company and had no real idea what was involved. But he knew that he wanted to get as much help as possible for the students. So, he decided to start a NonProfit.

"Besides," he said, "if the goal is to not make a profit – I mean, how hard can it be to *not* make money?"

People assumed the new group would be called The Brunch Bunch Foundation, but Greg quickly rejected the idea. He said his organization was going to do much more than take kids to brunch. One day, it would send kids to college. He wanted a name which reflected that broader vision.

The name he chose was *The 11-10-02 Foundation.*

11-10-02 stood for Greg's 30th birthday – November 10, 2002 – and his belief that people thirty and under can and should make a difference.

The unusual name caused a lot of people to scratch their heads.

"11-10-02 sounds like the combination to my locker," one kid joked.

More than the odd name, it was Greg's inexperience that people questioned. Nobody seemed to believe a 25 year old substitute teaching restaurant doorman could run something of this nature.

Nobody, that is, except his Grandma.

She told him all he had to do was the same thing he did all his life – *keep failing until you succeed* – and eventually the Foundation would prosper.

She said the real question was if he was willing to set aside his own goals like enrolling in law school, entering corporate America and writing books and films long enough to do it.

He looked her in the eye and said he was willing to spend as much time as necessary to build a Foundation that could change the world.

His Grandma smiled and said, "In that case, there's one more thing you need. This is going to take *so* long that your feet are going to hurt if you don't have a place to sit."

With that, she gave him her rocking chair.

The chair reminded Greg of the lesson he learned as a child, when he raised money for charity by reading books: As long as you are willing to spend the time, you can make a difference.

The recollection boosted his confidence.

His spirits were lifted even further when the Foundation received its first donation – a check for $100 – but it didn't take long before that excitement wore off and Greg realized his Grandma wasn't kidding.

Between the papers to fill out and the decisions to make, the Foundation took up more time than he ever imagined. Using his free time to get it all done wasn't an option because there wasn't any free time left. The only apparent solution was to clear something off his weekly schedule.

The step he took was a costly one.

He quit his job as a doorman at The Club. He learned a lot from his boss, liked his co-workers and enjoyed the customers, but he didn't have a choice. He needed more time to build the Foundation.

The extra hours on the weekends did help, but he still needed more time during the week when he could call people at work.

He decided to use his brief lunch break to do it. He knew ten minutes a day wasn't much, but he figured it was ten minutes more than nothing. Since he did not yet have his own cell phone, he searched around Blue Academy for a room with a phone where he could sit and make calls. Finally, he found a room on the 4th floor. It wasn't very big. It was the size of a walk-in closet – and half of it was taken up by a dishwashing bin – but it had a phone and a desk. So, Greg decided it would be a good spot. He declared it to be his "first office" and even hung up a BOARDROOM sign on the ledge.

It turned out there was one small problem.

It was the Lunch Lady's desk. That dishwashing bin was where she and her two co-workers cleaned the lunch trays each day. Nobody else entered that room without her permission. And *nobody* used her phone or put things up on her ledge.

Everybody expected her to kick Greg out, but she never did. She let him share her space for ten minutes each day.

On the surface, the two may have seemed to be an odd couple. They were different ages, faiths, genders, races and backgrounds. Nevertheless, they enjoyed each other's company. The Lunch Lady was amused by Greg's big dreams and admired his desire to help. In turn, he respected her work ethic. Her no-nonsense approach reminded him of his Grandma.

The extra ten minutes a day did help Greg get more done, and an article in the local paper about his efforts brought in a few donations.

Still, the young educator hoping to change the world was raising little more than spare change. When even the most basic supplies seemed too expensive, Greg turned to his new friend, The Lunch Lady, for guidance.

"Do the best you can with what you have," she said.

The advice added up to less than ten words, but it spoke volumes to Greg. After she said it, he treated everything he had like it was sacred.

A lunchbox was now a briefcase. Empty cereal boxes became filing cabinets. That brick he kept after the man beat up his car with it? It was now a paper weight. Even his refrigerator was used to store files.

(19) Make what you have be what you need

With a makeshift office of his own taking shape, Greg focused on how to spread the word about his new group. He decided the increasingly popular internet was the perfect way to start. Night after night, he sat at his computer and taught himself how to make a website.

The one he put together was not too fancy, but it was effective. More donations trickled in over the next few weeks. One of them was a check for five thousand dollars. When Greg saw it, he ran around in circles, waving the check in the air and shouting with joy.

Knowing there were people who believed so strongly in what he was doing, Greg felt motivated to look for ways to raise even more money.

Charlie suggested he write letters to companies who donate lots of money to charity every year and ask them for support.

Greg gave it his best shot. He spent hours filling out forms and writing grant proposals. Unfortunately, every response was the same. *No.*

As the rejections piled up, he felt like a high school senior all over again. He wanted to tear up the letters into little pieces, but his Grandma insisted he should do the exact opposite.

"We've been through this," she huffed. "Rejection is something to be proud of. You don't throw out letters like that. You frame them."

Accepting rejection letters was one thing. Turning them into art seemed like quite another. But Greg reluctantly did as she suggested. He framed a stack of the rejection letters and hung them on his wall.

It would not be the only time Grandma gave Greg advice that left him scratching his head.

When he continued to struggle in his efforts to raise the millions of dollars he hoped to raise, she told him, "Instead of trying to change the whole world, start with the world outside your window."

Greg was crushed. The way he figured, you don't tell someone to focus on small dreams unless you think they are unable to reach big ones.

A few days later, when he attended that Sunday's brunch, her words still weighed on his mind. As he sulked in silence, the other people at the table realized something was wrong.

After he explained why he was upset, one of the kids, Josh, brought up a good point to try and cheer him up.

"Your Grandma didn't say *stay* small. She said *start* small. You know, like you start small. Then, one day, maybe, your efforts get big."

Another kid (Trace) explained why it would be okay even if Greg's efforts never expanded at all. He noted that even superheroes like Batman focus their efforts on one city (Gotham) and not the entire world.

The more Greg thought about the insights shared by Josh and Trace, the more his Grandma's advice made sense. Instead of waiting until he raised enough money to fund big college scholarships, he decided to use what he raised so far to make a smaller but immediate difference to help kids in his local community.

(20) Before you try and change the world,
focus on the world outside your window.

Looking out his apartment window, Greg could see a variety of locations throughout The Green that might benefit from someone's support, but it took less than a minute for him to pinpoint where he wanted to start.

Blue Academy.

The school with the blue exterior wall had a special place outside his window – exactly four blocks to the west – and a special place in his heart. It was where he spent his first day as a substitute teacher, where those first two kids he took for shakes went to school and where he 'shared an office' with The Lunch Lady.

Admittedly, Blue Academy didn't look too impressive on the outside. The brightness of the blue paint on its exterior wall wore off long ago. Some of the windows were darkened. But Greg had been inside, and he was inside long enough to get far beyond that first impression.

He was especially struck by Principal Brooks and his staff. Sometimes, they weren't given enough books or supplies, but like The Lunch Lady said, they did the best they could with what they had. Even on the long days, most of Blue's teachers went out of their way to support each other. To Greg, they were exactly what educators should be – and everything he was trying so hard to be.

There was no doubt in his mind. Blue Academy was the school he wanted to help first. And sooner than he expected, he had a chance to do it.

One day, he asked the kind-hearted clerk, Ms. Boggs, if he could have a school t-shirt to wear around town. She said she appreciated his school pride, but there was no way to give him what he requested.

The school didn't have any school t-shirts.

Greg couldn't believe his ears. How can kids be expected to take pride in their school if they can't wear shirts with its name across the front? He knew right away this was a perfect chance for his organization to help make a small but lasting difference. He went home, designed shirts for the school, got the Principal's approval on the design and then ordered six hundred.

A few weeks later, Principal Brooks arranged a special assembly for Greg to unveil the shirts. The school didn't have a gym or theater. So, the event had to take place in the dimly lit first floor hallway. The custodial staff did the best they could to transform it into a makeshift auditorium. They brought out a podium and set out several rows of chairs. Due to the limited space in the hallway, only about half of the school's students were able to attend.

To an observer, it might not have seemed like an 'impressive' setting – for that matter, a few hundred shirts might not have seemed like a 'big' donation – but Greg didn't care. He was thrilled. His Grandma, Trace and Josh were right. Making a 'small' difference in the world outside your window is a big deal and a great way to start.

In the days that followed, the Foundation gave grants to other schools in that neighborhood – providing money for books, supplies and computers.

Each grant the Foundation gave out was named after one of Greg's favorite old instructors – from his 1st grade teacher to his professors from college. He appreciated them when he was a student, but he appreciated them even more now that he realized how hard it is to be a good teacher.

The kids seemed grateful for the help, but truth be told, more times than Greg could count, he felt the students were helping and teaching *him*.

When Greg was upset someone had not treated him nicely, it was a kid who put his feelings back in perspective with a note about a time when someone was "really not treated nicely" – when her cousin was killed. Greg was so struck by the note that he kept it in his wallet for months.

One day, the popular TV show, *Good Morning America*, announced plans to bury a Time Capsule that featured Greg's civic efforts. He was excited to share the news at school. Before he could say anything, though, a student pointed out he was wearing two different shoes. The entire room broke out in laughter. He was as embarrassed as could be. Instead of spending the rest of the day running around school and boasting about the television appearance, Greg did his best to stay glued to his desk where he could hide his feet. His Grandma loved the story so much that she ordered him to wear mismatched socks every day to ensure that a single glance at his feet reminded him how quickly and easily he had been humbled.

These were just two examples of many. Time and time again, Greg left school at the end of the day with a new lesson he learned from the kids.

After the speech at Blue Academy, Greg got invited to speak at other schools and events. Each time, he opted to speak from the heart instead of writing a speech. His friends often joked that, given how much he rambled, he was asking for disaster. On stage, though, he spoke slowly and clearly. He never went longer than the time allotted to him. And no matter the size of the audience, he felt surprisingly at home in front of them – his insecurities and self-conscious nature giving way to his lifelong desire to tell stories that impacted the way people think.

Of all the invitations Greg received, none were sweeter than when he was invited back to his old high school to speak at an all-school assembly. It was the triumphant return he imagined for years.

At least, it was supposed to be.

When Greg arrived at Mortimer Dowhill, all of his old teachers who still worked there came up to greet him.

All his old teachers, that is, except one.

Avery P. Welton. The man who wrote that 'recommendation' letter.

When Mr. Welton entered the room, he took a seat without saying a single word. To add insult to injury, he wouldn't even look at the podium.

In an instant, Greg felt his old anger bubble back toward the surface. Part of him was tempted to shout at Mr. Welton until they turned off the microphone, but he resisted the urge to do it.

Looking out at the smiling faces of his other old teachers who had always been kind to him, looking out at the impressionable teenagers sitting beside them, he couldn't do it. The school asked him – and trusted him – to send a positive message to those students. No matter how upset he was, that's what he was going to try and do.

Instead of bringing up Mr. Welton and The Letter, he spoke instead about all the good things he remembered about the school and the teachers there who had such a positive influence on his life. Then, he talked to the kids about diversity and service – using his brunch program and foundation as examples for them to think about.

In his heart, Greg hoped that taking the higher road might lead to something positive. Perhaps, Welton might finally apologize after all these years. Unfortunately, after the speech, the man still did not say a word to his former student. Not to admit he was wrong when he wrote The Letter all those years ago. Not to congratulate Greg on his success in college. Not to commend him for making a difference in his community. Not to thank him for avoiding mention of The Letter during the speech. Not even to say hello.

Not one single word.

Greg headed back home feeling sick about the experience.

Then, when he was *this close* to being convinced that his effort to stay positive had been pointless, he found out about Clifford.

A sophomore at MDCR, Clifford reached an inspiring conclusion after hearing Greg's speech. He too wanted to make a difference, and he too wanted to do it now instead of later.

In the days that followed, without telling anyone, Cliff wrote letters to companies all over the country. He asked them to help Greg send kids to college.

The boy's efforts did not succeed, but the mere fact that he tried was enough to brighten Greg's spirits when he found out about it. Something positive came out of his decision to stay positive when he spoke at his old high school after all.

It didn't take long for the ripple effect to continue.

When a junior at another high school named Fitz heard about what Cliff did to try and help others, Fitz decided to do something, too. He assembled a jazz group and announced plans to throw a concert with all the proceeds going to The 11-10-02 Foundation. Over the next few months, Fitz and his pals practiced songs, passed out fliers and told everyone they knew about the show. They even got their principal to let them use the school auditorium.

As Greg sat in the audience, he listened to the concert and observed the people of diverse backgrounds who came together to appreciate great music. He nearly burst with pride. Going back to his days in Louisiana, he found great value in bridging divides. To hear Fitz and his jazz band use their talents to do exactly that was, well, music to his ears.

The future of the fledgling Foundation seemed bright, but Greg's personal path was not getting any easier. He continued to face one roadblock after another. In the fall, that obstacle became his feet.

Seemingly out of nowhere, Greg found himself unable to walk without pain. The doctor said the problem required surgery on his left foot.

At first, Greg viewed the news that he needed to spend a few days off his feet as a vacation. He expected a wheelchair to be like the Big Wheel he rode as a boy. He even insisted on – literally – wheeling himself home from the hospital after the surgery. He was quite the sight to behold – laughing and singing as he inched his bandaged body down the street.

Once he finally made it home and the medicine wore off, he got a rude awakening. Three days in a wheelchair proved to be one of the most eye-opening, humbling experiences of his life. In the process, he developed a newfound respect for the strength possessed by people who deal with physical obstacles every day of their lives.

The operation didn't stop Greg's streak of brunches – he had the kids wheel him to the restaurant – but it was a close call. And it wasn't the only one. He overcame every obstacle imaginable to keep the streak of weekly brunches alive. There were blizzards, heat waves and the day his car broke down ten minutes before a brunch. Not to mention, birthday parties, weddings and anniversaries. Sometimes, he was sick or just plain tired. But, in the end, nothing ever got in the way of The Streak.

Two months later, Greg had the same operation on the other foot and was back in a wheelchair for three more days. Within a week, he was back on his feet, but he no longer could run around as freely as he once did.

His Grandma insisted it was a blessing in disguise.

She said, "If you have to walk slower, it takes you longer to get somewhere. The longer it takes you to get somewhere, the more you appreciate getting there once you finally do. And besides, if it makes you stay off your feet, then you get more time to work on things like your art."

As always, she was right.

He spent more time on his sketches. Over time, they kept improving. The kid who was unable to draw a straight line had slowly but surely taught himself to draw portraits that were practically lifelike.

The drawings got so good that, one afternoon, a repairman broke into Greg's apartment to see the originals framed on the walls.

"I wasn't going to take anything," the man insisted, when questioned later. "I just wanted to see if he drew anything new since I fixed his sink."

Most of the time, Greg drew leaders throughout history and his favorite characters from film. As a result, his portrait of a real president was framed right alongside his portrait of an actor who portrayed a president in a movie.

Like so many other aspects of Greg's life, his wall of framed drawings became a blend of fiction and reality.

The more time he spent on his art, the more those lines seemed to blur. As he drew the pictures, he got carried away into the worlds of the people he drew – imagining their friends, their families, their fate.

As it turned out, art did more than flex the muscles of Greg's imagination. It also helped him become a little more patient. He spent weeks on each drawing – perfecting every hair, wrinkle and freckle – before framing it and putting it up on his wall.

For a guy who rarely wanted to sit still and silent, art seemed to be what the doctor ordered.

More than anything, art helped him think about perspective. When he drew a mouth, for example, he had to think about two things at once. Besides focusing on how the mouth looked, he also had to consider how that piece fit into the larger puzzle – the face – he put together.

Over time, he realized the lesson applied to more than art. In life, there are always those two processes at work – what you are doing at the moment and how that moment factors into the bigger picture.

(21) A well-drawn mouth can still turn a portrait into a cartoon if it is drawn next to a nose instead of beneath it.

Greg's most prized portrait was his drawing of Martin Luther King, Jr. He framed it on the wall by his desk. It reminded him of the time he spent sitting on his mattress in the dorm hallway in Louisiana, King's poster on the wall behind him. In turn, that memory helped Greg keep his own still-secret *Dream* fresh in his mind.

In between drawing portraits, Greg worked on the Foundation's logo. He tried to come up with one ever since the group's inception. A year and a half later, he finally created the symbol he wanted.

Greg insisted it was perfect, but others were not so sure. In fact, most of his friends openly laughed when they saw what he drew.

"It looks like something done by a fifth grader!" one friend howled.

They were only teasing him, but in a roundabout way, the logo *was* drawn by a fifth grader.

The images within the logo represented the things Greg saw years ago outside his childhood window. From top to bottom, the images in the logo represented The Silhouette Man swing set, the Ladder Horse, the three bushes (the ovals) and his puppy's grave beneath the middle bush (at the base of the middle oval). The triangle that connected all the dots? It represented the tent Greg put up in the yard on the weekends.

Harvard Charlie could not believe his eyes when he saw it.

"Are you crazy? You weren't supposed to draw a picture of what you saw out your window when you were a little boy. You were supposed to come up with a serious image that represents the Foundation."

Charlie was trying to help, but his words upset Greg greatly. As kids, the two lived parallel lives. The same schools, same camps and (it was expected) same bright future. Somewhere along the way, though, their lives drifted in different directions. Charlie followed the path that was "expected" – Ivy Leagues, then corporate America, and now, a top business school. Greg, on the other hand, detoured off the fast track and blazed a much less certain trail that included stops in Louisiana, The Club and The Green.

Along the way, their philosophies on life diverged greatly, too. Charlie did believe in giving back, but it was something he planned to do *after* he became independently wealthy. Greg, on the other hand, believed it was important to make a difference and leave a legacy *now* – even if that meant delaying his own financial pursuits in the meantime.

Their daily lives (and bank accounts) reflected those different paths and philosophies. Charlie wore tailored suits, carried a briefcase, traveled the world and took his dates to fancy restaurants. Greg wore mismatched socks, carried a lunchbox, rarely ventured beyond the world outside his window and took his dates to local diners with coupons he clipped out of the paper.

Greg didn't mind that their philosophies and paths veered in such different directions. His frustration stemmed from the fact that his father reminded him on a daily basis that the Harvard graduate was living the sophisticated life he "could be and should be" living. So, instead of taking Charlie's comment about the logo for what it was – advice from a friend – Greg saw it as the guy he was "supposed to be" telling him what he was "supposed to do" – and he couldn't stand it.

Grandma had little patience for his complaints.

She huffed, "I don't care what your father says. Charlie is Charlie. Greg is Greg. The only person you oughtta compare yourself to is the guy in the mirror. If you're doing better than you were doing a year ago, then you're doing fine. That's the only competition that matters."

(22) The only person you should compare yourself to is…yourself.

As always, her advice helped. Ironically, though, in this particular instance, Greg really shouldn't have worried about what Charlie said.

His logo was a lot more complex than his old friend or anyone else realized. Yes, its different parts were inspired by what Greg saw outside his childhood window, but that was only Phase One. Every part of the logo also symbolized different parts of the brunch mentoring program.

The Three Ovals were not just three bushes. They also represented three glasses – symbolizing the day Greg and two kids had milkshakes. The three shakes that eventually led to the start of The Brunch Bunch.

The Tombstone represented the tombstone in Greg's old yard. It also represented what he first learned from his brief friendship with the puppy buried there: Seize the chance to get to know new friends at brunch today because there's no guarantee they'll still be there tomorrow.

The Ladder represented The Ladder Horse in the backyard. It also represented what the kids hopefully learned at brunch. The ladder's five rungs symbolized five principles that lead to a successful future: ethics, effort, etiquette, education and (positive) environment.

The Silhouette on top of the ladder represented The Silhouette Man swing set in Greg's old backyard. It also represented the idea that if a kid took the lessons taught at brunch to heart, then he or she will have climbed the ladder's five rungs and made themselves (and the program) a success.

The Triangle represented the tent Greg used to put up in his backyard. It also represented a mountain, and the belief that it was good to make a big deal out of something small – to make a mountain out of a molehill – if it's done for a positive reason. And that's what Greg had done with The Brunch Bunch – turning a couple shakes into a full-fledged program.

As Greg's feet healed, he continued to help others whenever possible – whether it was hosting the weekly brunches now on the verge of their three year anniversary, bringing more friends with him to volunteer at The Center, surprising a hard-working music teacher with a grant for more instruments, or dressing up as Santa Claus on Christmas Eve and delivering gifts to a church and other locations in and around The Green.

He hoped his efforts inspired other people to do something, too.

And, once in a while, that's exactly what happened.

In some cases, people were inspired to support his goals – signing up for a brunch, volunteering to come with him and visit seniors at The Center, or making donations to The 11-10-02 Foundation.

Sometimes, they were Greg's friends. One of his old camp counselors in Wisconsin sent him a desk. Sometimes, they were total strangers. A woman in Oklahoma sent a fax machine.

In other cases, people heard about Greg's efforts and were inspired to set new goals of their own. More than once, he got a note from someone who said his story inspired them to go back to school to be a teacher.

As the weeks passed, Greg's story kept spreading in more directions.

An English teacher assigned his story to her classes in conjunction with *Schindler's List* directed by Steven Spielberg and *Night* by Holocaust

Survivor Elie Wiesel. Another school had Greg and Wiesel – the substitute teacher and the Nobel Peace Prize honoree – speak on the same day.

The President of the United States sent The Brunch Bunch Kids a letter to encourage them to continue their efforts to celebrate diversity. A month later, Greg and his Grandma graced the cover of *Senior News*. A New York fashion magazine even did an article about what he wore – running a photo of his mismatched socks.

Despite the unusual twists and turns, Greg was determined to stay focused. With that in mind, he returned to his hometown to announce a special grant in honor of one of the teachers who tried especially hard to help him when he was a boy. Then, he traveled to Bailey's hometown to speak at *his* old school and announce a grant from the Foundation that would help the students there.

The grant wasn't the only honor Greg named after the friend he met at football camp nearly a decade earlier. He decided to name The 11-10-02 Foundation's first college scholarship in Bailey's memory, too.

With the money in place to fund it thanks to another $5,000 gift, all Greg had to do now was decide which student got it. To help narrow the field, he contacted eleven schools and told them they could each nominate two seniors. In turn, the nominees were asked to prepare applications.

To pick the winner, Greg asked a dozen friends to review applications. They agreed to do it, but judging was no easy task. In fact, it was so hard that they could not choose between two of the finalists.

Fortunately, before Greg had to break the deadlock, somebody solved the problem for him. One judge was so impressed by the nominees that he made some calls and came up with the money for a second scholarship. The Foundation not only had its first ever Scholar. It now had two!

This was something Greg pictured for years. It definitely called for a celebration. He chose a popular restaurant in the area to be the site of the party. The Brunch Bunch ate there a number of times over the past few years. Their food was delicious, and their staff always treated the group with dignity and kindness. Given that The Restaurant had a separate banquet room that could cater to hundreds of people, it seemed to be a perfect fit.

On a personal level, Greg was excited about more than just the location.

Twenty years after setting foot in a theater for the first time, seven years after he passed up the chance to study film in Europe, and four years after his brief trip to California, Greg still yearned to tell stories that changed people's lives. This event was his chance. It was going to be a *show.*

He wasted little time getting started with its production.

The first decision was easy. For the musical entertainment, Greg invited Fitz and his pals to be the band – out of appreciation for the concert they put together a few months earlier.

With that out of the way, Greg focused on the trophies. Some of his friends couldn't understand why it mattered. Trophies are trophies, they said. The winners will be happy to get one, no matter what it looks like. After all, their real prize was the scholarship.

Greg listened politely, but he insisted it was an important decision.

He said, "Every great story has a symbol. Willy Wonka, he had those golden tickets. Forrest Gump, he had shrimp. I gotta have one, too."

He spent hours scouring catalogs and looking for a unique design. None of them met his approval. Finally, he designed his own trophies using *unwashed milkshake glasses.*

Greg's friends thought he was nuts, but he insisted it was perfect.

"First of all," he told them, "they symbolize the day I took the kids for shakes that led to all this. More importantly, the whole point is we're trying to show that everything and everyone has value. What better way is there to prove that than by turning moldy, dirty milkshake glasses into trophies?!"

After getting Mr. Goldberg the Trophy Maker to agree to make the trophies (despite the horrible smell), Greg turned his attention to selling tickets. Since there was no budget for invitations, he walked around the neighborhood and talked to everyone he passed.

Not too many were impressed by the 'Gala' he was promoting.

After hearing Greg's sales pitch on the street, one observer said, "It seemed like a cute little event, but it certainly wasn't a *Gala*. A Gala is a fancy affair on a Friday or Saturday night at a big hotel. This was going to take place at a restaurant on a Sunday. There were no sponsors, no invitations and the band was a bunch of kids. I'm sorry, but that's no Gala."

Ticket sales were hardly Greg's only source of stress. He had become, to put it nicely, fed up with much of the media.

To be clear, when they wrote about him or The Foundation or talked about him or it on TV, they always said nice things – and the positive attention did help the organization attract new supporters. The issue was that some of the reporters used labels like *underprivileged* and *disadvantaged* to describe the students, and it frustrated Greg to no end.

Having discussed the issue with his students, he realized the labels were the result of a double standard – *'When's the last time you saw a headline like 'Overprivileged kid wins spelling bee?'* – and unfair – *'Why does the media get to decide what a privilege is?'* – and vague – *'Less fortunate than who?'* – as well as hypocritical – *'Why write an article praising someone's efforts to break stereotypes if you're gonna use some of those stereotypes in the story?'*

He complained on a daily basis until, finally, his Grandma spoke up.

"You're giving me a headache," she huffed. "If you've got something to say about the media, do what they do – write it down."

He did as she told him. He wrote down his feelings about stereotypes and labels. When he was done, he submitted his essay to the local paper as a guest column (and kept submitting it until they finally agreed to run it).

He knew his column in and of itself wouldn't solve the problem, but it was, at least, something.

Of all the lines he wrote, his favorite was the one he repeated to the students again and again for the past three years. The same line his Grandma repeated to him all his life.

The most important word in the world is your name.

It was with that line in mind that the guest column included something that had not seen the light of day very often since Greg was a boy. His full name – unique middle name, Forbes, included.

Having spent so much time telling kids to take pride in their names, he decided it was time to embrace his own.

**

Greg had evolved from a shy child into a young adult bursting with confidence. Even socially, he finally came into his own. The boy who stuttered when he saw the pretty girl with blue eyes was now a grown man featured in magazines as one of the most eligible bachelors in the city.

Hot! Hot! Hot! declared one headline.

At first, Greg thought the articles – and the bags of mail that followed – were all a bit silly, but given the teasing he took as a kid, it did not take long for the affection to go to his head. And like always, it took even less time for him to be humbled right back to reality.

When being prepped for one of the magazine photo shoots, Mister Eligible noticed some black dust in the air.

"What's that?" he asked the hair stylist.

"Powder," she replied. "It's to cover up the shine from your head."

He didn't understand what she meant. She picked up a mirror and showed him. When he saw what she was pointing at, he was mortified. A clump of his hair was missing.

Charlie said, "It wasn't the end of the world for him to lose some of his hair at a young age, but you still had to feel bad for the guy. He was such a scrawny kid for so long. After all those years in the gym, he finally felt like he had reason to feel good about the way he looked. Then, suddenly, chunks of his hair started to fall out. If it wasn't one thing, it was always another."

Greg tried to block the whole thing out by focusing on volunteering even more in the community.

In the meantime, word of those service efforts continued to spread.

That summer, he flew to Washington D.C. for an annual event where a handful of people were recognized for making a difference on the 'local' and 'national' levels. Greg was one of the 'local' honorees.

The trip turned out to be one of the most memorable experiences of his life. In the span of three days, he attended a reception with U.S. Senators, a dinner with the likes of former astronaut John Glenn and a ceremony in the Supreme Court with Justice Sandra Day O'Connor. He also met the President of the United States and even walked the President's dog around the West Wing of the White House.

Despite the brief nature of the trip, Greg's Presidential Dog-walking episode was only one adventure of many. In another instance, he strolled into the train station, unaware that a major motion picture was in the process of being filmed. In another case, he took a wrong turn down a hallway and interrupted a reporter doing a broadcast for the nightly news. In yet another case, he misread his schedule and showed up to a hotel suit-and-tie breakfast *in his pajamas.*

"I'm very sorry. When it said 'breakfast, suit and tie' in the schedule, I thought I was supposed to come down for breakfast and *then* go put on a suit and tie," he explained to the shocked (and amused) organizers.

While a hundred guests in suits and dresses giggled, Greg sat down and ate two plates of pancakes before going upstairs to his room to change.

It was fun to 'rub elbows' with Senators, the President and a Supreme Court Justice, but the other 'local' award winners – 36 adults and four kids – were the ones who truly embodied Greg's favorite kind of public service. They were living proof of what he believed since he was a child reading about Harriet Tubman: You don't need to be an elected leader or CEO to make a difference in the community.

Greg was especially inspired by one of the four student honorees. Jarrett was an an eleven year old boy from Kentucky. He spent much of his young life battling cancer, already losing his hair and one leg in the process. Yet, instead of dwelling on his own problems, the boy founded an organization to brighten up the lives of other kids facing obstacles.

Greg marveled at Little Jarrett's positive attitude. The boy had so much inner strength that he continued to have the confidence of a heavyweight champ, even as his physical condition worsened. For Greg, it was a humbling reminder that there's a lot more to life than some pain in your feet or a shiny reflection off the top of your head.

> *(23) Don't judge a person by what you can see.*
> *Don't judge a person by what you cannot see, either.*

Less than two weeks later, it was the last Sunday in June, and the Gala at The Restaurant was a few short hours away. Despite having no sponsors, no invitations and no planning committee, Greg somehow sold every ticket.

With hundreds of people expected for the big show, he wanted to spend the afternoon double-checking all the details, but it was a luxury he didn't have. Gala or no gala, Sunday afternoon still meant it was time for brunch.

And this one was going to be special.

Greg's 172nd brunch in a row was going to be the very last one.

He had promised his parents that he would enroll in law school or get a corporate job once he fulfilled his goal of helping a student pay for college. If he chose a school or job out of state, the streak of weekly brunches was bound to end.

Rather than drag it out, he decided to bring everything to an end on one unforgettable day. This was going to be that day.

For the final brunch, Greg thought about a reunion of the hundreds of people who came to at least one outing over the years. As the day grew closer, he had a change of heart. He decided it was more fitting to end the streak of brunches the same way it started.

One man, two kids and three milkshakes.

Shortly after noon, without any fanfare, Greg and two kids – Trace and Josh – made the short walk to get a bite to eat, gulp down some shakes and bring the streak of brunches to a simple and quiet end.

At least, that was the plan.

When they arrived, the restaurant refused to serve Greg.

Not that he should've been surprised. After all, he had not chosen some random location. This was Dorothy Keyser's Place.

Two years earlier, when Greg first brought The Brunch Bunch to different restaurants around the city, he convinced every spot in town to give the group a discount – except for Keyser's Place.

Rather than accept the possibility that DKP's could not afford to do it, or that they already supported their fill of worthy causes, or that they simply didn't like to support any causes in general, Greg took it personally. He was convinced the head of Keyser's Place was trying to undermine the success of his beloved mentoring program.

It was the same insecurity Greg displayed again and again ever since Mr. Welton betrayed him nearly a decade earlier. If someone – especially someone in a position of authority – didn't fully support his plan, he became convinced they were actively trying to ruin it.

When he felt that way, he almost always lashed out with long, rambling notes oozing with self-righteous anger.

Rose said, "It was painful to watch because you knew the letters weren't going to accomplish a thing, other than upsetting the people who received them, but you also knew there wasn't much we could do to get him to stop. After the situation with Mr. Welton, if Greg saw someone interfering with his dreams – or anyone's dreams for that matter – he felt like it was his personal responsibility to speak up."

His friends warned him that there would eventually be a price to pay.

Greg's business-wise friend, Abby, told him, "I know it's important to you to express yourself, but some people have long memories. Sooner or later, you're going to want something from one of them, and they're going to say no because they're upset about some dumb letter you wrote years earlier."

That's exactly what happened with Keyser's Place. After they didn't offer a discount to The Brunch Bunch like other restaurants did, Greg wrote a note ripping Keyser's management. Two years later, they still remembered the sting of his words.

Forget the discount. Now, they wouldn't even serve him at full price.

The Brunch Bunch Kids always observed the positive relationship between Greg and the people who ran the restaurants they visited. Not knowing Greg's history with Keyser's Place, Josh and Trace were stunned to see him denied service.

They were even more surprised by his response. The same man who protested even the smallest injustice walked away from this one with a whimper – taking the boys to another restaurant a few doors down and acting like nothing happened.

Trace said, "I didn't know what to make of that. I guess I thought, maybe, with this being the last brunch in such a long streak, he just wanted to end it on a positive note. So, when they wouldn't let him in, maybe he dropped it as quickly as possible, so it didn't ruin the big day."

Three hours later

The sold-out Gala was slated to start at twenty-five minutes after six. Yet, when six o'clock rolled around, Greg was nowhere to be found.

When he finally showed up at The Restaurant – only a few minutes before dinner was to be served – he apologized and said that he lost track of time. In his rush to get there, he said he also forgot the seating chart – so the Gala guests had to sit anywhere they found an open seat.

It might have seemed like Greg was a disorganized mess, but things were actually going according to his secret plan. In truth, he never made a seating chart – hoping the Gala could be like the brunches where people sat next to strangers and walked out with new friends. He arrived at the last second on purpose so nobody could say there was time for him to run home and get the seating chart he 'forgot' to bring with him.

The guests dressed nicely but nothing too fancy – except for a kid named Rockefeller ('Rocky' to his friends). He was decked out in a tuxedo.

"If it's a Gala to you," the boy said to Greg, "then it's a Gala to me."

Greg smiled warmly at the remark. Rockefeller was one of his favorite students – polite to classmates and teachers, hard-working in school and out of it, plus he had the unique kind of name that a guy with the middle name 'Forbes' could appreciate. Once Rockefeller and the other guests chose their seats, they ate to their hearts' content as Fitz and his band mates filled the air with the sound of jazz.

When the delicious meal was done, everyone looked at Greg. They assumed he would be first to speak, but they were in for a surprise. Josh and Trace – the students he brunched with earlier in the day – approached the microphone and announced *they* were hosting the show.

The program began with three tributes to the late friend after whom Greg named the Foundation's first scholarships. First, one of Bailey's relatives gave a speech about him. Then, a representative of the football camp where Greg and Bailey met a decade earlier announced they were putting up a plaque in the locker room – a plaque that talked about life being about more than winning games. Finally, a rep of the college that Bailey planned to attend a decade earlier had he lived announced that the school decided to create and fund a special one-time scholarship and name it after Bailey – and they were going to let Greg pick the winner of it, even though none of their representatives ever met him before the night of the Gala.

It seemed to be an amazing leap of faith – the audience was shocked – but it would be just one of many surprises to come.

After the crowd settled down, Trace said it was time to pay tribute to the supporters who helped make the Foundation a success. Everyone expected a bunch of wealthy donors to get recognized, but that wasn't what occurred. The honorees were people who usually aren't appreciated in public – like the lady who printed the Foundation's first business cards and the accountant who helped with the financial work.

After a few more awards and grants were handed out, it was revealed that the next surprise was for Elliott, the long-time Brunch Bunch kid who caught the foul ball at a baseball game.

The Principal of a highly selective high school – a high school that turned Elliott down when he applied two years earlier – approached the microphone and explained to the audience that Greg recently spoke at an assembly at their school.

"In the weeks that followed," she said, "a number of our students got to join The Brunch Bunch. As a result, many of them met Elliott. And one by one, they returned to campus and said the same thing: The school would be an even better place with Elliott in it."

The Principal paused, smiled and said, "And we agree."

Two years after Elliott was rejected, the high school he dreamed of attending let him in – and gave him a scholarship to boot.

As Elliott hugged the Principal, Greg watched on with pride. It was a moment that showed the true potential of the bridges he created. Make no mistake, there was nothing unique about people using their connections to help a friend. In fact, it occurs every day. What was unique was that, in this case, the people doing it were teenagers and the friend they chose to help was from a different part of town.

It wasn't changing the game. It was changing who gets to play.

After Elliott sat down, the co-hosts returned to the podium and said it was time to do what everyone was waiting for – give out the Foundation's first ever scholarships.

Right on cue, the double doors to the banquet room opened and three students walked in. Each one held a Milkshake Trophy.

While most of the guests were distracted by the look (and smell) of the unusual trophies, the volunteers who served as scholarship judges were surprised by something else – the number of them. There were only scheduled to be two scholarships, but there were three trophies.

Charlie leaned over to his date and whispered, "I don't know what's up Greg's sleeve, but some kid in this room is in for a big surprise."

Charlie was right.

After the first two Scholars were honored, Rockefeller went to the microphone to announce the name the third honoree. As the audience watched on, the kid in the tuxedo peeled the sticker off the front of the third trophy and discovered the third Scholar was someone he knew all his life.

Himself.

According to the co-hosts' copy of the script, that was the grand finale.

So, while Rocky's mom sobbed with joy, Trace and Josh approached the podium to thank everyone for coming and to say goodnight. Suddenly, Greg headed toward the microphone to speak for the first time all night.

"Sorry to interrupt," he said, "but I think their script is missing a page or two because according to my copy, we're only getting started."

He paused, then added, "First up is the live auction. People kept telling me that every real Gala has one, so we're gonna have one, too."

The audience sat up on the edge of their seats. What valuable item was going to be auctioned off to raise money? An exotic trip?? A diamond??

Uh, not exactly.

The "valuable item" turned out to be a framed copy of *Senior News* – the magazine featuring Greg and his Grandma on the cover.

The audience laughed loudly, but Greg insisted it was no joke.

"This isn't any ordinary magazine cover, folks. This one is signed by the world's greatest Grandma!" he declared. "And if the world's greatest athlete's autograph is valuable, the world's greatest Grandma's autograph is valuable, too! We start the bidding at five thousand dollars!"

Charlie recalled, "I know that already seems nuts, but I'd like to point out his Grandma didn't even sign her name. She signed the word *Grandma.* Think about it. It's like Babe Ruth signing *Athlete* instead of *Babe Ruth* on a baseball."

Greg waited for someone to make the opening bid of five thousand dollars, but nobody even bid a buck. You could hear a pin drop. The excitement building all night came to a sudden and awkward halt.

Greg refused to budge.

Finally, just when it seemed like the silence was going to last forever, a stranger in the back of the room ran up to the podium, said he felt inspired by the night, wanted the autograph and was willing to donate $5,000 – matching the largest gift the Foundation ever received – to have it.

The entire room was stunned – including Greg's Grandma, who hollered that the winning bidder was "crazier than Greg!"

Little did she know, she hadn't seen anything yet.

As soon as things calmed down, Greg said he had two more surprises. First, he turned to his right and surprised Josh, the co-host, with a five thousand dollar scholarship. Before anyone could catch their breath, he turned to his left and surprised Trace with one, too!

The audience rose to their feet to give a standing ovation. The two boys' moms burst into tears like Rocky's mom did moments earlier.

The scholarships for the co-hosts seemed to be the perfect ending, and everybody assumed it *was* the ending.

But Greg declared he was not done. He said he had an announcement to make. He said it had to do with his "immediate future."

He explained how he had promised his parents he'd get a corporate job or go to law school after he helped a student go to college. It seemed like he was giving a farewell speech to the Foundation's supporters.

Then, suddenly, he changed topics and told the crowd how he was denied access to a restaurant earlier in the day. He said that proved there was still much more work to be done. He said the brunches in particular and the Foundation in general had to continue. To make that possible with his schedule, he planned to substitute teach for yet another year.

Greg's parents were shocked, but believe it or not, their son still had one more surprise to share. It was the biggest one yet.

When the room quieted down, Greg asked all of the students who were *not* there to get scholarships to rise. There turned out to be fifteen in all.

He told them he made a list of criteria based on attendance, grades, conduct and civic service. Each of the fifteen who could meet that criteria throughout the rest of their time in high school would get $5,000 for college – a staggering $75,000 if all fifteen met the criteria!

Then, and only then, Greg smiled and said the show was over.

As the crowd headed toward the exits, still reeling from all the twists and turns, Charlie approached his old pal to get some answers.

"How'd you come up with the cash for those extra scholarships given out tonight?"

Greg replied, "Remember how I was going to finally take a salary for running the Foundation?"

"Yeah," said Charlie.

Greg shrugged and said, "I decided not to take it."

Charlie was at a loss for words. By his own admission, his *self-worth* was tied to his *net worth*. So, he could not wrap his head around such a massive financial sacrifice.

And it was not the only thing that confused him.

"*You* were denied access to a restaurant? You're Mister Brunch Bunch. You get along so well with all those restaurant managers. Which one wouldn't serve you a meal?" Charlie asked, convinced there was a catch.

"Keyser's Place," Greg replied.

It was exactly as Charlie figured.

He wagged his finger at Greg and said, "You know what I think? I think you didn't want to walk away from all this, and you wanted an excuse in case your parents questioned you. So, this morning, you purposely went to the one and only restaurant where you might get a hard time. This way, you could come here tonight and tell everyone that you've got to keep fighting the good fight. Getting turned away from Keyser's Place, that wasn't a change in the script. It was part of it."

Charlie looked like he was proud of himself for 'figuring out' what was going on, but Greg was not overly impressed. Like the director of any compelling show, he wanted to leave the audience with at least one unanswered question. *A cliffhanger* that made them think. And even if Charlie did unravel one mystery, there was still another that left him stumped: *How in the world would a substitute teacher come up with $75,000 in case all fifteen of those students met the criteria for scholarships?*

How could Greg be so sure that Charlie didn't know the answer to that? Because there wasn't one yet. Greg had no idea how he was going to raise all that money.

As it turned out, the solution came to him before sunrise.

**

When Greg arrived home from the Gala, he was so tired that he headed straight to bed without even taking off his suit.

At least, he tried to go to bed.

He had so many thoughts running through his mind that he was unable to sleep. He put his shoes back on and went for a walk to get a milkshake.

Three blocks down the road, he came across a bar/restaurant that was still open. Unfortunately, they didn't have shakes on their menu.

As he turned to leave, a customer called after him.

"Hey," the man said, "My name is Lou. I'm a doctor. I go to the gym on weekends. You take the kids there every Sunday. Come meet my girlfriend, Maddie, and tell her about what you do. She'll be inspired."

Greg was tired, but he agreed to do as Lou asked (in return for a grilled cheese sandwich). After hearing the story, Maddie said she was *so* inspired that she wanted them to go with Greg for shakes right then and right there. When a waitress, Sugar, heard what was going on, she took off her apron and said she wanted to go with Greg for a shake, too!

Off they went, in the middle of the night, a doctor, his girlfriend (an artist), a waitress and a substitute teacher in search of some milkshakes. A few blocks down the road, they came upon a popular twenty-four hour restaurant called Tempo Cafe and headed inside.

For the next thirty minutes, the four sat around a table – telling stories and enjoying milkshakes. As they did, Greg decided he wanted to keep their glasses as souvenirs. He walked over to the cash register to speak with the manager on duty and make the unusual request.

The manager was in no mood to deal with a goofy customer. He turned down Greg's request and told him to go back to his seat. While Greg tried to change his mind, a man walked in Tempo's front door. He immediately thought Greg looked familiar. When he overheard the conversation about milkshake glasses, he quickly put it all together.

"Milkshakes?!" he hollered. "That's why I recognize you! You and your friends take kids for milkshakes! I've read about you in the paper!"

The man was *so* excited to see Greg that he ran over to the table, sat in Greg's seat and *finished Greg's shake.*

Sitting around the table in the middle of the night at a twenty-four hour cafe, Lou, Maddie, Sugar and the Complete Stranger laughed and joked and gulped down the rest of the shakes without giving a single second's thought to the fact that they were from different races, cultures and backgrounds.

After watching with a mix of amusement and pride, Greg eventually pulled up a chair and rejoined the table.

Shortly after 4 A.M., the five new friends went their separate ways. As he walked back to his apartment, four glasses dripping a trail of vanilla behind him, Greg smiled from ear to ear. And not just because the manager changed his mind and let him keep the glasses. At that moment, he wasn't even smiling about the success of the Gala a few hours earlier.

As he made that pre-dawn walk from the cafe back to his apartment, he smiled because he suddenly came up with the idea to help him raise the money he pledged to raise during the Gala's grand finale.

And this wasn't any ordinary idea cooking in his head. He was certain it was the world's greatest idea!

Greg decided if people were that excited to have a shake with him, he could charge people five grand to do it. (In reality, his plan was to sit down for a shake with anyone who donated $5,000 – a fun way to celebrate the funding of a new scholarship – but there was no telling Greg that. He insisted he was 'selling' the world's most expensive milkshakes.)

He figured it was a sure-fire way to come up with the money to fund those scholarships. As word spread, though, most people thought his foolproof idea was nothing more than proof he was a fool.

At first, they seemed to be right.

No matter how hard Greg tried, he couldn't 'sell' a single $5,000 shake.

In the meantime, something else *was* sold – the building where he lived. Greg was reluctant to pack up and move, but he soon saw a silver lining. He spent nearly four years trying to change the world outside his window. Perhaps, a new apartment with a new window would give him a chance to take on a new set of challenges.

He chose an apartment in another high-rise building just a few blocks away from his first one. As soon as he moved in, he put the rocking chair by the window and explored his new view.

All the way to the left, he could see The Green – the community where he spent much of his time teaching over the past several years. All the way to the right, he could see The Big Hotel – one of the fanciest places in the entire city. There was less than a mile between the two, but Greg knew it might as well be a thousand. The world of The Green and the world of The Big Hotel rarely if ever merged together.

Almost instantly, Greg knew what he could do to change his new view for the better. He tried to build a bridge between The Benches in Louisiana. He tried to build a bridge between students and adults from diverse backgrounds through the brunches. Now, he dreamed of building a bridge between The Green and The Big Hotel. To connect the dots on his left and on his right. To create an opportunity for those two worlds to co-exist together instead of side-by-side.

He stayed up night after night plotting ways to make it happen, but it wasn't the only reason his new view kept him up late.

As fate would have it, Greg could also see the local movie theater out his new window. The theater's neon sign was a painful nightly reminder of the lifelong dream he sacrificed to help the kids reach their dreams.

Fortunately for Greg, there was great news to keep his spirits high. He 'sold' his first $5,000 shake – to a professional hockey legend, no less. The two drank them at the hockey star's annual charity golf outing. Not surprisingly, a sports icon drinking a $5,000 milkshake on a golf course made headlines in a bunch of papers. The next thing you know, other people 'ordered' a $5,000 milkshake of their own.

A law firm ordered one for their boss for Christmas. A banker ordered a shake for his wife for Valentine's. And on and on it went.

Greg's milkshakes became so popular that a carpet cleaning company even featured him and his Grandma in an ad campaign. According to the ad, Grandma hired the company because "Greg won't sit at the table when he drinks his milkshakes and keeps spilling on my carpet."

After a few months, Greg raised the 'price' up to $7,500 per shake – adding whipped cream to justify the increased cost. He seemed to be pushing his luck, but the 'orders' kept coming.

Each time Greg met one of the 'buyers' for a shake, he saved their used glass so it could be turned into a trophy to go along with the scholarship named after the person who 'bought' it (or the company they represented, or their relative if they drank the shake in someone's honor or memory).

As unlikely as it might have seemed when Greg first came up with the idea, so many people donated money to have one of his shakes that he was able to cover the scholarships he pledged to fund if any of the still eligible students met the criteria he announced at the Gala – and there was even money to spare.

He knew exactly how he wanted to use the rest.

He wanted to help the students who tried to help others. He gave college scholarships to Cliff, the teenager who wrote all those companies, and Fitz, the one who led the band.

**

While Greg's Foundation blossomed, his physical condition worsened. He was sleeping less which meant he was exercising less which meant the muscles were slowly fizzling away. To top it off, his hair continued to fall out in clumps. Finally, he shaved off what was left. A year after being featured in magazines as a young, strong, healthy bachelor, Greg was bald, weak and exhausted. He tried his best to stay positive, but he found it difficult to look in a mirror and feel good about what he saw.

Determined to snap out of the funk, Greg came up with a way to get back in good shape and raise money for The Foundation at the same time. He announced plans to run in his first ever marathon and line up people to pledge donations to help fund scholarships for each mile he ran. His friends admired his goal, but they were not so sure he could do it.

"You've never run in a marathon," said Arthur, an experienced runner who lived one floor above him. "What makes you think you can do this?"

The answer was one Arthur probably should have seen coming.

"If Forrest Gump can run non-stop for a couple years. I think I can handle running a couple miles one time," Greg said with a shrug.

Obviously, it made no sense to think it was possible to complete a marathon based solely on a made-up movie character's ability to run non-stop for several years – but the issue turned out to be moot.

A few weeks after deciding to enter the 26.2 mile race, Greg had to have two more operations on his feet. He was depressed about the setback, but his Grandma didn't let him wallow in self-pity for long.

She huffed, "We've already been through this. If you gotta stay off your feet, work on something you can do sitting down – like your art."

He knew better than to argue with his Grandma. He did as she instructed and worked on his drawings. He also spent more time focusing on his logo.

Back when he first drew it, people thought the logo was 'too simple'. What they did not know at the time was that the logo had more than one meaning. It even had more than two. According to Greg, there was a third meaning. He decided this was the perfect time to unveil it.

In Version One, the logo represented the things Greg saw outside his childhood window. In Version Two, it represented the different parts of The Brunch Bunch (BrunchBunch.com) program. Version Three was going to be all about scholarships – new scholarships, to be exact.

In Version Three, *The Ladder* symbolized the belief you should never underestimate the strength of those who help themselves up the ladder of success. With that belief in mind, the new Ladder Scholarship would assist students who were so busy working to, for instance, help their family pay the bills that their grades suffered a bit because of it. They only had B or C grades, but they clearly had a straight A work ethic.

The Tombstone represented the philosophy that the only thing that lives forever is a legacy – and that in order to leave one, you first must create one. With that in mind, The Legacy Scholarship would help a student who carried on Greg's legacy: breaking barriers, building bridges and making a difference at a young age.

The Three Ovals once again depicted three milkshake glasses. But this time, instead of representing the day that Greg took two kids for shakes and the woman sitting next to them moved her purse, the ovals symbolized the Milkshake Glass Trophies given to the new Scholars.

Greg intended to get to work creating the other two pieces of the puzzle – the scholarships based on *The Triangle* and *The Silhouette Man* – but his schedule was so packed that it was difficult to find the time to do it.

Then, 9/11 happened.

On September 11, 2001, America suffered one of the worst attacks ever. That Friday, anxious to get away from the TV coverage he watched all week long, Greg accepted an invitation to attend a special service promoting peace and harmony. Afterwards, he went to dinner with five of the other attendees. Four of them were people he did not know.

Not surprisingly, they talked about the terrorist attacks while they ate. It was an impossible subject to avoid. The unique thing was that they were not talking much about what happened. Instead, they talked mostly about what could be done in response.

One of the people, a young building developer named Jonathan, thought about it from a real estate perspective. What could be built on that space where the Trade Centers stood to prove the nation still stood proudly? Greg, on the other hand, thought about it from a teacher's perspective. What could be done to show students that you can turn anything – even something this negative – into something positive?

By the time the bill came, the two men (who never met before that night) found a way to combine their ideas. The plan they came up with was a contest where high school students create designs to rebuild the space where the Trade Centers stood and write essays explaining how their designs captured the strength people in New York showed in the aftermath of 9/11.

The idea was well-received.

A teacher named Mr. Mack said, "I always tell students that a building, if you do it right, can tell a powerful story. This was a chance for them to do exactly that – design buildings that tell powerful stories."

It was also a chance for them to win a college scholarship. The students who won the contest were going to receive The 11-10-02 Foundation Mountain Scholarships – named after the mountain (triangle) in the logo. In this instance, the mountain represented the idea that it is good to build something big and positive out of something negative.

**

In the weeks that followed 9/11, a number of schools invited Greg to speak with their students. One invitation brought him to Kentucky.

He looked forward to his first visit to the Bluegrass State, but under the circumstances, he wasn't too sure what kind of a response to expect. From his time in Louisiana, he knew how nice that people in another part of the country could be. On the other hand, in the wake of the terrorist attacks on 9/11, it would be very understandable if even the kindest of people were reluctant to roll out the welcome wagon for a stranger.

And yet, that's exactly what the people of Kentucky did.

When Greg got lost and asked a woman for instructions, she gave him her map. When he asked a resident where he should eat dinner, she didn't merely recommend a restaurant. She joined him for the meal. When he strolled into a local courthouse and asked if he could check his e-mail there, a man rose from his seat and offered up his desk. It was only as Greg left that he found out the man who let him borrow his computer *was the judge.*

The way everyone welcomed a stranger with open arms would've made Greg feel good at any time. To see them do it shortly after 9/11 astounded him. As he wrote in a guest column for a paper at the end of his trip, "After what I experienced the last three days, I reached a conclusion. The world would be a better place if everyone was a little more Kentucky."

While Greg was there, he got the chance to spend time with Little Jarrett and his family. The young boy with cancer put Greg's physical problems back into perspective. How could Greg complain about the pain in his feet when Jarrett only had one leg? How could Greg complain about being bald at the age of 28 when Jarrett looked that way since he was ten?

During the trip, Greg also paid a visit to the hospital where Jarrett's organization brought toys to sick children. Seeing the program the boy put together in spite of his own obstacles, Greg was reminded yet again that a person's true strength has nothing to do with how big and strong they seem on the outside.

That reminder helped give him the idea for the final new scholarship.

In Version Three of his logo, The Silhouette Man stood for the idea you should never measure a person's strength by the shape of their silhouette or shadow. With that in mind, The Silhouette Scholarship was going to help a student who achieved great things despite having to deal with physical obstacles along the way. A kid whose true strength came from within.

The boy from Kentucky was not the only student helping out the community at a young age. Clifford – the student from Greg's old high school – continued to make a difference, too.

On his first day of college, Cliff went for a walk and found a school where he could volunteer. Over the next few months, he returned there on a regular basis and brought some of his new college classmates with him. If the process sounds familiar, it's with good reason. Cliff was trying to trace the civic steps Greg took during his freshman year a decade earlier.

Before long, university officials found out about Cliff's efforts. They were proud of him and curious about what inspired him. When he told them about Greg's speech a couple years earlier, it was not long before they invited Greg to fly out there and speak to their students. The speech was scheduled for a Thursday evening.

To show Cliff how much he admired his volunteer efforts, Greg stayed through the weekend and held that week's brunch there. It was the first one he hosted in another city. The "adults" were Greg, Cliff and some of Greg's friends who happened to live in that area. The "kids" were a handful of the grade school students Cliff tutored on a regular basis.

At first glance, it appeared to be like all the previous brunches. Adults and kids eating a great meal and getting to know each other – talking about college and careers, learning about people from different cultures and backgrounds. But it was no ordinary brunch. Instead of turning to the adults and asking questions, Cliff was now answering them from younger kids.

Right before Greg's eyes, a student grew up and became a mentor.

In the process, by 'paying forward' the kindness, Cliff brought the whole experience full circle. And it turned out that was all Greg was waiting to see.

After 243 weeks, he announced his streak of brunches was over.

Cliff was stunned to learn he helped inspire the end of such a long streak by tutoring kids at a local school and joining them at brunch, but he shouldn't have been that surprised at all. You can never underestimate the power – or the ripple effect – of a simple act of kindness.

If the end of the streak of brunches was a fitting way to celebrate Greg's 29th birthday, which happened to be that very day, then the events of that night were icing on the cake.

Inspired by Greg's story, Cliff's roommate (Perry) wanted to bring people of different backgrounds together, too. He decided Greg's birthday was the perfect excuse to do it. While Greg and Cliff were with the group at brunch that afternoon, Perry invited people to join Greg for dinner that night.

Perry's efforts were more successful than he imagined possible.

Forty complete strangers gathered together for dinner, on a few hours notice, to celebrate the birthday of a guy they didn't know.

Greg was grateful for Perry's efforts and particularly touched by the restaurant that was chosen. A place called John Harvard's.

"We would've taken you to the actual university," Perry said with a grin, "but that was a little bit out of our budget."

For two hours, those who were in attendance set aside any apparent superficial differences and made new friends.

When the event was over, they presented Greg with a special gift. A menu.

That's all it was – a menu – but there was no telling Greg that. As everyone went their separate ways, he walked back to his hotel, clutching that menu with the word *Harvard's* across the front like it was as important as an actual diploma bearing the same name.

**

As word spread that The Brunch Bunch Week Streak ended, people tallied up the statistics. Over 700 people from 32 different states and six continents attended at least one of the brunches. More than any other number, of course, it was the length of The Streak that caught people's eye.

Greg was *twenty-four years old* the day he took two kids for shakes and *twenty-nine* when he took a break 243 weeks later. A commitment of time that was impossible to deny – and almost impossible to imagine.

As one kid, Trace, pointed out, "I graduated from middle school, went to high school, graduated high school and went to college, and the man *still* never missed a single week of brunch. It was pretty amazing."

The pats on the back were well-deserved, but the more compliments Greg received for maintaining The Streak for such a long period of time despite all of the obstacles in his path, the more he seemed to believe he could overcome *any* obstacle without *any* help from *anyone*. As usual, it didn't take long for him to be humbled back to reality.

One night, Greg and his photographer friend, Guy, went to see Brunch Bunch Kid Elliott play basketball at his new school. After the game, Greg tried to take a picture with Elliott. Unfortunately, the camera wouldn't work.

"Want some help?" asked Guy.

"I can do it," Greg said snidely. "It's a camera, not rocket science."

Guy watched with amusement as Greg shook the camera, pushed its buttons, checked the lens, then shook it again with increasing frustration. Finally, he gave up and declared the camera unfixable.

Guy chuckled, yanked the aluminum flip-top off of Greg's soda can, inserted it in a particular place in the camera and said, "Say cheese."

Greg laughed him off, insisting that could not possibly do the trick. But he was wrong. FLASH! It worked like a charm.

It turned out the piece of the camera that covers the batteries fell off. Apparently, there needed to be a substitute of some kind to hold the batteries firmly in place and act as a conductor of the current.

In the process of finding that substitute and inserting it in the right place, Guy solved the problem. The professional photographer also reminded Greg of a valuable – and important – lesson to remember in the future.

(24) Life is a challenge, but it is not an exam.
It is okay to ask for help from someone who knows more than you.

People thought the end of The Streak meant Greg might finally take a vacation, but it was not to be. Now that schools were nominating students for the new scholarships, he was eager to devote his time to lining up judges to pick the winners. He spent his first brunch-free weekend in nearly five years with his Grandma, but then it was back to volunteering.

(25) The best reward for hard work is more hard work.

The Legacy Scholarship Judging Panel was the easiest to assemble. Given the personal nature of the scholarship – the fact that it was going to be given to a student who carried on the legacy Greg was trying to leave – he decided to select the winner himself.

For the other three kinds of scholarships (The Ladder, The Mountain and The Silhouette), he planned to ask thirty friends – ten per panel – to serve as judges and pick the winners.

Until, one phone call from Lambert Grover Wakefield changed all that.

Some time earlier, Greg read an article in which Wakefield described himself as someone who stayed grounded despite his great success. The well-known CEO claimed he always made time to help others.

Having learned his lesson about not asking for advice, Greg looked up Wakefield's office number to set up a meeting.

Each time he called, however, the CEO's assistant turned him away – saying her boss was in a meeting, out of town, or unavailable.

Finally, one time Greg called, the assistant said his timing was perfect.

"Stay by the phone, and he will call you in two minutes," she said.

Greg excitedly paced back and forth, rehearsing all the questions he wanted to ask. Right on cue, the phone rang.

Before Greg could ask anything, the CEO made a statement of his own. "You should have taken the hint. I don't talk to people your age."

Greg tried to respond, but it was too late. Mr. Wakefield already disconnected the call. The man had called back just to hang up.

(26) Never make a hero out of someone you do not know.
Admire only the qualities within them about which you are certain.

Determined to turn a negative into a positive, Greg vowed to prove Mr. Wakefield was the exception and not the rule. He wanted to demonstrate most prominent executives *were* willing to lend their time and wisdom to support the efforts of young people. Greg said he would prove this by looking up the names of very successful people, calling them at their offices and convincing them to serve on one of his new Scholarship Boards.

Greg's friends understood why he was mad, but they insisted he was only setting himself up for more disappointment. They said busy corporate executives would never take his call, let alone agree to give their time to help out a tiny foundation run by a substitute teacher they never met.

Stubborn and defiant as ever, Greg always replied the same way.

"Apparently, you've never heard of Brantley Foster."

Brantley was a young college graduate working in the mailroom of a company in New York. He convinced a bunch of top investors and executives to back his ideas. At that point, he took over the company.

It seemed to be an inspiring example for Greg to follow. Of course, there was one problem. Brantley didn't actually exist and neither did the big-shots who supported his ideas. They were all characters in a movie.

As always, that mattered little to Greg. If Brantley won over top executives, then he figured he could, too.

Despite the doubters, he moved forward with his plan.

As expected, some of the people he called turned him down. Others never replied at all. But Greg was not worried. He took the rejections in stride and made more calls.

The persistence eventually paid off.

One by one, a few said yes. Then, a few more. And then, a few more after that. When all was said and done, the young substitute teacher shocked everyone. He convinced thirty of America's leaders in fields like finance, athletics, law and business to come aboard one of his tiny organization's scholarship committees.

Mr. MacMillan, the head of a major toy company, was among those who signed up.

He said, "Was it the largest charity on Earth? Of course not. But as someone who started from nothing, I don't care about that. I don't worry about how old you are, nor do I care about the size or scope of your project. If you have work ethic and passion, you'll have my respect. Furthermore, I appreciated that he wasn't asking for my money. Everybody asks for my money. He was asking for my time and my opinions."

Once MacMillan and the others were on board, Greg divided them into three smaller groups – one to select the Ladder Scholars, one to choose the Mountain Scholars and one to pick the Silhouette Scholar.

The meetings were scheduled for three Thursdays in a row in late May and early June. In the meantime, the nominees had a couple extra months to finish up their applications, and Greg had some extra time to make sure he planned out every last detail of the three Board meetings.

His decision to spend the extra time focused on those meetings was understandable. These were going to be three very important meetings for the young Foundation and its founder. Still, there was little doubt he should have spent the extra time on vacation.

He was exhausted. He even suffered from sudden sleeping spells.

Sometimes, it was a cause for humor. On a date, he fell asleep headfirst into a bowl of soup. Usually, it was much more serious. One night, he collapsed in the shower, hit his head and cut it open.

His body was not the only thing showing signs of wear and tear.

The rocking chair was, too.

In fact, Greg spent so many hours rocking in the chair that he *rocked a hole right through it.* The splinters of the seat fell to the ground.

He was scared to tell his Grandma what happened to her chair, but she smiled when he gave her the news. She called the splinters of the chair a "symbol of his work ethic" and told him to save them.

He did as she instructed – framing them on his wall above the desk – but he was still sad about the chair's demise. After spending thousands of hours together, he saw the chair as more than a mere place to sit. Much like The Silhouette Man and The Ladder Horse from his childhood backyard, The Rocking Chair had become a trusted companion and friend.

Unfortunately, he didn't have much time to mourn his loss.

With all four scholarships created (The Legacy, The Mountain, The Ladder and The Silhouette) and the judges' meetings around the corner, it was time to plan another party to honor the eventual winners.

Given the success of the first event, Greg's friends said he should bring everyone back to The Restaurant, but he had another location in mind.

The Big Hotel.

He loved everything about the first Gala, but a number of people still teased him every time he referred to it as a *Gala.*

"It was a banquet," they insisted. "Restaurants host banquets. Hotels host Galas."

Greg knew he should pay them no attention, but he couldn't help himself. He wanted to prove he could put on a *real* Gala like sophisticated socialites do. He wanted to prove he could be *one of them.* He was certain that a successful event for 500 people in the 10,000 square foot Regal Ballroom at The Big Hotel would silence all the doubters for good.

And what's more, like he dreamed when he first moved into his new apartment, he wanted to build a bridge between The Green on his left and The Big Hotel on his right. This seemed like the chance to do it.

His friends admired his desire to think big, but it seemed to them that a substitute teacher with a tiny Foundation was way out of his league trying to put on a full-fledged Gala at The Big Hotel – and they told him so.

Greg insisted he was up to the challenge and wasted no time trying to prove it. In a matter of days, he got a new website to promote the event, lined up a big company to be the evening's title sponsor and persuaded a local magazine to help publicize it with a free advertisement.

For the event itself, to make sure it ran smoothly, Greg set up a Planning Committee comprised of a dozen friends willing to volunteer their time. With their help, he was certain the event would be a piece of cake to pull off, but it soon became clear he went from one extreme – refusing to ask a friend (the photographer) for help – to another extreme – demanding his friends on the Planning Committee devote every waking minute.

No matter what his friends on the Committee did, Greg wanted them to do more. No matter how much time they spent, he told them to spend more. He didn't ask nicely, either. Day after day, he sent them angry notes and barked orders at them through the phone. His philanthropic goal was noble, but he was *so* determined to reach it, that he lost sight of the feelings of the people who volunteered their time to help him do so. Not surprisingly, his approach left his friends feeling disrespected and unappreciated.

One by one, they started to quit. After a few weeks, most of the Committee disappeared.

(27) How many people are on your side when you set a goal is much less important than how many are still there when you reach it.

While Greg focused his attention on the event where the new Scholars were going to be honored, other people focused their attention on him.

Zeta Beta Tau honored him as its youngest ever Man of Distinction. A short time later, he received a special civic honor given to one person in the entire nation each day.

Then, in the spring, a community college called PSC invited Greg to be its Graduation Speaker.

PSC officials said they also wanted to give Greg an honorary degree – making him the youngest person to receive one in the school's history.

Honorary or not, it would be the first college diploma Greg ever held in his hands. So, he proudly declared he would treat it like a real degree.

His father, Mark, was not amused.

He griped, "An honorary degree is not actually worth anything."

Despite his father's grumblings, Greg continued to treat the upcoming event like it was going to be his actual college graduation. When PSC officials told him the Graduation Speaker always wears a special set of colors around the neck to recognize where he or she went to college, Greg decided not to wear any colors at all.

"Only the cap and gown like my fellow graduates," he insisted.

As the day drew near, Greg requested tickets. He wanted to invite his family to attend the ceremony. After all, that's what 'graduates' do.

The school granted the request, but his parents would not go, his sister could not go, and his Grandma said she was too ill to make the trip.

Determined to still put the tickets to good use, Greg invited some of his Foundation's Scholars to take their place.

Graduation Day

While the five 11-10-02 Foundation Scholars took their seats in the back row of the auditorium, Greg took his seat up on stage. Decked out in his cap and gown (with his mismatched socks peeking out the bottom), he looked around at the thousands in attendance and smiled from ear to ear.

It was exactly as he always dreamed.

Halfway through the ceremony, the President of PSC went up to the podium to introduce Greg.

At first, it seemed like a traditional introduction for a ceremony of that nature. PSC's President talked about the speaker's accomplishments and awards he received in the past. Until, he mentioned something that took the audience – and especially the five Foundation Scholars – by surprise.

This was the first college graduation Greg ever attended.

He not only skipped his own – *he'd never been to anyone's*.

When the introduction was over, Greg took a deep breath, rose from his seat and approached the microphone. He had no notes, but he didn't need any. This was a moment he pictured since he was a boy.

He began the speech by telling the audience about his lifelong effort to draw and what his Grandma always said about straight lines.

Then, he reflected on the struggles and obstacles he and his 'fellow graduates' faced to get to this moment and this stage – how it turned out their lives had not been much of a straight line, either.

"But," he concluded, "the thing is, knowing what I know now, I don't regret it, because my Grandma was right. A straight line is the shortest distance between two points, but it's definitely not the most rewarding."

He paused for a moment to let his words sink in.

As they did, he asked The 11-10-02 Foundation Scholars in attendance to stand. As 2,000 people turned around to look at the five students in the back of the auditorium, Greg told them how proud he was to have them there and how important it was that they "cross a stage like this one" some day down the road.

Then, he turned his attention back to PSC's new graduates sitting up front – men and women who worked so hard to reach this moment in their lives. He told them to be as proud of the obstacles they overcame as they were proud of the goals they achieved.

"And," he said in conclusion, "I hope you are as proud to be a part of this graduation class as I am."

When he finished his remarks, the audience rose to their feet and applauded. PSC's President later said it was the first standing ovation for a Graduation Speaker during his tenure.

Normally, at this point, a school rep approached the podium to present the honorary degree. Before the ceremony, though, Greg begged officials to make an exception and let him line up with his 'fellow graduates'. He desperately wanted to do what he never did before – *cross the stage.*

The graduation planners granted his unusual request, but they didn't want to mess up the alphabetical order of the actual graduates.

They told him, "When the time comes, file in at the back of the line."

Greg eagerly agreed to follow their plan.

And now, that time had come.

One by one, the graduates took their turn. Their name was called. They crossed the stage. They fulfilled their dream. Their relatives in the audience snapped photos and shed tears of joy.

Meanwhile, at the back of the line, Greg anxiously waited his turn. After all these years, and so many ups and downs, he was only a few minutes away from holding a college degree for the first time.

Moment by moment, he inched closer to the front of the line. Until finally, every other name was called. Every graduate crossed the stage but him. It was now his turn.

As the audience cheered and his name echoed through the rafters, Greg crossed the stage, took his degree, hoisted it in the air and shouted with joy.

The idealistic boy who once hoped to finish top in his class from the Ivy Leagues was now a thin, frail, limping, tired, bald man who graduated last in his class with an honorary degree from a community college.

It was the happiest moment he could remember in his entire life.

(28) What you're holding in your hand at the end of a journey
is not as important as the walk you took to get there.

After the event, Greg took the photos to his Grandma's apartment. He could not wait to show her. These were the 'crossing the graduation stage in a cap and gown' pictures he promised her six years earlier.

As soon as he arrived, he excitedly flipped through the stack. He gave his Grandma a play-by-play description of each picture as he did.

"This is me in my cap and gown before I went on stage! This is me giving the speech! This is me crossing the stage and getting the degree! I kept my promise. Here are your pictures!" he shouted with joy.

It was a striking image to an impartial observer.

Greg was a grown man. The CEO of a Foundation. He had received a number of the country's most prestigious civic honors. His efforts to be more than a bystander had been recognized by Presidents and chronicled in a Time Capsule buried on national television.

Yet, in the quiet of that living room, it was clear: At his core, he had not changed since he was a little boy. More than anything in the world, he just wanted to make his Grandma proud.

**

When prominent business leaders joined The Foundation's Scholarship Boards, it opened a lot of eyes. It also created some challenges.

The primary issue was that the executives who agreed to serve on the three Scholarship Boards were *so* busy that there was no way their schedules allowed them time to review all the nominees' applications.

After giving it some thought, Greg came up with a solution. He assembled a Junior Scholarship Board responsible for sifting through the nominees and selecting the finalists. That way, when the three Scholarship Boards met, they only had to review ten nominees apiece.

Everyone liked the idea. Until, that is, Greg announced the Junior Board would be a bunch of teenagers.

The decision to give young people this opportunity struck many as a mistake.

"You can't trust a bunch of kids with something like this," one skeptic said.

Greg disagreed. As far as he was concerned, the idea was consistent with his goals. In fact, it was his goal. He wanted to prove young people can do a great job if they're given the chance to do it.

Despite the critics, he moved forward with the plan. He rounded up a dozen students from a dozen schools to serve on the Junior Board.

When the time came, the group met in a back room at a local restaurant and reviewed the applications. Two teens from Greg's hometown – a girl named Claire and a boy named Alex – were put in charge.

The group took its role seriously. In fact, they took it so seriously that their meeting lasted late into the night.

With the finalists selected, it was time for the Senior Boards to meet. The Ladder Board went first.

At precisely ten minutes past six, Greg walked into the conference room where the ten executives were gathered, took his seat at the head of the table and said in the most confident of voices, "Ladies and gentlemen, it's time for us to get down to business."

Decked out in a perfectly-pressed suit, a handful of America's most successful leaders sitting alongside him, for one fleeting moment, the substitute teacher looked and felt like a real CEO.

But after crossing the stage with the students of PSC, it no longer mattered to him quite so much if anyone else saw him that way. He no longer wanted to be *one of them*. He wanted them to be *one of us*.

It was right about then that everyone noticed Greg's BOARDROOM sign. It was the same old, faded sign that he hung up years earlier in the Lunch Lady's room at Blue Academy. He brought it to the meeting and put it up before the Scholarship Board Members arrived.

"I wasn't stepping into their world. They were stepping into ours," Greg said with pride, when asked why he brought the sign with him.

Seven days later, the Mountain Scholarship Board had its meeting. Seven days after that, the Silhouette Scholarship Board took its turn. Each time, Greg displayed his beloved BOARDROOM sign for all to see.

As the final meeting came to an end, he walked out the door with a feeling of great satisfaction. With the applications reviewed and the judges' votes cast, he was now *thisclose* to fulfilling the third version of the logo.

With his civic goal so close to being achieved, Greg thought more than ever about his Grandma. He knew he never would have been able to get so far without her support. After all, she was the one who gave him that chair and made him believe a substitute teaching restaurant doorman could build a philanthropic organization from scratch. The one who taught him how to deal with rejection. The one who urged him to work twice as much as the kids who seemed twice as smart. The one who convinced him it was okay if he couldn't draw straight lines.

Day after day, for nearly three decades, Grandma was there for him. It might have been tough love, but it was unconditional love, too.

In return, Greg repeatedly tried to show his appreciation. He called almost every day. He visited regularly. Over the years, he arranged everything from a surprise party for her birthday to autographs from her favorite TV stars. And yet, Greg always felt like he still had not done enough to thank her. He wanted her to understand that she was the World's Greatest Grandma.

Whenever he told her that, she wagged her finger and said, "That's what *you* think. You go ask ten other kids, and you'll get ten other answers. Everybody who has got a Grandma will say their Grandma is the best one."

Greg nodded politely, but her words did not sway him. There were many super grandmothers, but his Grandma was in a league of her own. No matter what it took, he wanted to convince her of that. A few days after the Scholarship Board meetings, he came up with the perfect way to do it.

His idea was to create a website, www.WorldsGreatestGrandma.com. It would host a competition to find the World's Greatest Grandma.

The contest was obviously a farce – Greg planned to name himself the one and only judge – but he moved forward with the plan.

He submitted an essay to nominate his Grandma. A minute later, he declared the 'competition' closed. Then, the judging panel (just him) read the (only) nomination and selected the winning Grandma (his own).

Charlie laughed, "How was that *possibly* fair?"

"Every essay was judged fair and square," Greg snapped.

Charlie pointed out the obvious – there was only one essay and it was the judge who submitted it – but Greg was too excited to care. In fact, he was so proud he thought he was going to burst! He could not wait to see the look on his Grandma's face when he told her that she was, officially, the World's Greatest Grandma!

But he never got the chance.

A few hours later, that very day, she passed away.

Greg never felt anything so painful in his entire life. The sadness and grief caused by his Grandma's loss and its timing consumed him.

Hoping to clear some of the thoughts from his head, he sent an open letter about his Grandma to his friends and wrote a guest column about her for *Senior News*. As fate would have it, that effort to vent about the single most negative experience of his life gave birth to something positive.

In the days that followed, people around the country responded to what he wrote about his Grandma. Some of those responses included donations to the Foundation in her honor.

When Greg took a moment to add up all the checks, he realized there was enough there to fund an extra scholarship.

A few days later, he met with his Grandma's caretaker on a bench behind the building where his Grandma lived for the past decade. For twenty minutes, the two sat quietly, gulping down milkshakes and toasting the creation of this new and unexpected scholarship.

**

Greg felt the pain of his Grandma's death for years to come.

In the short term, he distracted himself by focusing on the Gala.

The event was shaping up to be a night to remember.

Four tables worth of items were lined up for the night's silent auction. A bunch of great companies signed on as sponsors. There were even going to be invitations this time around – thousands of them.

Ironically, the invitations created a new problem. Somebody had to stuff, seal and stamp all the envelopes.

Fortunately, a bunch of students volunteered to do it. All of them were helpful, but one kid in particular stuck out from the others.

A few months earlier, A.C. Lucas was nominated for one of the Ladder Scholarships, but the Board did not pick him.

A big, tough football player, A.C. hardly seemed the type to take defeat with a gracious smile. Yet, here he was, offering to help stuff the invitations to the party honoring the students who were picked for the scholarships instead of him.

Knowing firsthand how hard it was to cope with rejection as a high school senior, Greg wanted to do something special for A.C. So, he gave him two free tickets to the Gala.

A.C. was not the only student looking forward to the big event.

A week before it took place, Elliott gave Greg a gift.

The soon-to-be high school graduate said, "It's the foul ball I caught at that game. That was five years ago now. I've kept it all this time. Now, I want you to have it. It'll bring you good luck next week."

Greg could not wait for 'next week' to arrive. While the Gala itself was a source of excitement, he was ready for the planning process to be over. It had not been fun. If anything, it had become a chore.

For all the great things The Big Hotel was, he realized there was one thing it wasn't and never could be.

The Restaurant.

When Greg dealt with The Big Hotel's representatives, he felt like a 'customer'. The people who worked at The Restaurant made him feel like a 'friend'. Given his personality, that made a world of difference.

The Big Hotel was magnificent, but it just wasn't the right fit.

The irony was deep.

Yet again, just like when he left Louisiana to go to Vernon Froehmann Whitfield University, Greg chose a great location (The Big Hotel) for the wrong reason and gave up a place he loved (The Restaurant) in the process.

After years of dreaming and months of planning, the big night at The Big Hotel finally arrived. At a quarter to six, hundreds and hundreds of people paraded inside the Regal Ballroom.

As Greg envisioned, the event served as a bridge that united people from both sides of town. For one night, they all came together under one roof.

As they stepped into the massive, elegant ballroom, the Foundation's longtime supporters could not believe how much things had grown. But if any of them were concerned Greg lost sight of how, why and where he started, those concerns quickly disappeared.

Instead of some famous band, Fitz and his friends still played the music. The table centerpieces were milkshake glasses hand-painted by Blue

Academy students. Instead of inviting a high-profile celebrity, Greg tapped Rocky – the 'kid in the tux' at the first Gala – to be the night's keynote speaker. And yet again, a couple of teens were chosen to host the show. This time around, it was Cliff and two girls, Brandie and Hannah.

And Greg was still, well, Greg. He showed up to the event three hours early – which was good – *but he was wearing his pajamas.*

"I wasn't thinking about my clothes. I just didn't want to be late," he shrugged. "You all start dinner without me. I'll go put on my suit."

In truth, it was another well-planned excuse for Greg to avoid being present if and when guests complained about the lack of a clear seating plan.

He couldn't stand seating charts.

People always asked ahead of time to be seated with people they already knew. They valued the 'familiar'. But he wanted them to sit with strangers and make some new friends.

Right on schedule, Greg returned in his suit a few minutes before the post-dinner program started on stage.

The program began with the presentation of awards to some supporters of the Foundation. As with the first Gala, the awards went to supporters who usually get overlooked – like the man who made the trophies.

There was also a gift lined up for the Lunch Lady and her two co-workers – dinner for three at one of the nicest restaurants in the country!

With the awards and gifts handed out, they moved on to the scholarships.

The first was the one created and funded in memory of Bailey by the university he planned to attend had he lived. Greg was given the chance to select the recipient. In the end, he couldn't choose between two nominees. Luckily, the school reps decided he didn't have to pick. They agreed to give scholarships to both students!

The good news kept coming.

A few moments later, it was announced that the Foundation was so proud of how A.C. handled rejection – offering to help stuff invitations for the Gala – that a brand new scholarship was created for him!

Then, it was Rocky's turn to be surprised (again). In the middle of his speech, the 'kid in the tuxedo' noticed the head of his university walking toward the stage. She said the school was so impressed by Rocky's freshman year that they were going to match the Foundation scholarship given to him last time!

With those surprises out of the way, it was time to give out the special scholarships to the kids who met Greg's challenge laid out at the first Gala.

The challenge succeeded on multiple levels.

Of the fifteen students, three of them received jobs from people they met through the process. Three received internships. Two got computers. Eight received grants from the Foundation. To top it off, three of them managed to meet all the criteria and earn $5,000 scholarships.

The parade of surprises and scholarships brought smiles to the faces of everyone in the room. Everyone, that is, except Greg. The man who pictured this night for years – and scripted it out right down to the final word on the final page – anxiously paced in the back of the room. Like any director, he wasn't going to relax until the final curtain fell.

Next up was the live auction. The items up for bid included a stay in France, a Total-Traveler cruise and a diamond!

Once the auction was complete, it was time to give out the last set of scholarships. These were the ones that represented the four symbols in Version Three of the logo. One by one, the scholarship winners were all called on stage. The Legacy Scholarship was first. It went to Elliott. The Foul Ball Kid was on his way to college! The Ladder Scholars were honored next. Then, the Mountain Scholars took their turn – their post-9/11 designs on display for all to see.

After the Legacy, Ladder and Mountain Scholars were honored, there was one thing left to do – reveal who was standing on top of the mountain in the logo. It was time to give out the Silhouette Scholarships.

The first was named after Little Jarrett. The boy from Kentucky was living proof that a person's strength couldn't be measured by their size or shape. The scholarship went to a young man named Dennis, who graduated high school with all A's while being confined to a wheelchair.

The second Silhouette Scholarship was named after Greg's Grandma. Despite being unable to walk or see well in her final days, she remained as strong as ever. The scholarship went to a young man named Dan. Despite a horrible accident that shortened his arms and forced him to spend his life on crutches, he managed to graduate high school at the top of his class.

Dennis and Dan were exactly what Greg pictured when he created the Silhouette Scholarship. The two boys had a level of confidence and strength that shattered any stereotype about so-called *handicapped* kids.

As the duo basked in the glow of their inspiring acceptance speeches, the audience rose to their feet and gave them a standing ovation.

The Silhouette Scholars had been honored.

The picture was complete.

Or so it seemed.

As Hannah, the co-host, stepped forward for the show's conclusion, an audience member ran on stage with a Milkshake Trophy and declared there was a third Silhouette Scholarship to give out.

Hannah peeled off the sticker covering the base of the trophy. When she did, she discovered it was her name engraved on the front.

Her hands and legs shook as she approached the microphone.

"I, uh, oh my gosh, wow, I can't…I don't…I mean, I, uh…"

The surprise left her – literally – speechless.

The audience was touched, but they were also confused. The Silhouette Scholarship was supposed to be for students like Dennis and Dan who dealt with physical obstacles. At first glance, Hannah didn't appear to have any physical limitations or challenges.

And that was the point.

Hannah's physical obstacle was *inside.* As a young girl, she had an operation on her heart that forced her to spend much of high school studying from home. Her obstacle might have been hard to see, but it was there.

Hannah provided yet another powerful reminder that people need to look beyond the surface to know someone else's complete story.

And just like Dennis and Dan, Hannah had not let her obstacles stop her from success – graduating near the top of her class despite what she endured.

The image of the Silhouette was yet another irony in a story filled with them. In the third version of Greg's logo, the man standing on top of the mountain with his arms raised in victory represented three people instead of one. One of them – Dennis – couldn't stand. One of them – Dan – couldn't raise his arms. The third – Hannah – wasn't a man.

It may have taken Greg nearly three decades, but as Dennis and Dan and Hannah triumphed on stage, he did what the doubters always said was impossible. He made The Silhouette Man come to life.

In the process, *The First Thirty* took on another meaning. Between the students honored at the first Gala and the ones honored at the second Gala, Greg helped his first thirty Scholars.

Perhaps even more ironic was the identity of the people who raised the money to fund the scholarship for Hannah. Unlike so many of the other scholarships funded by corporations, or at least by wealthy individuals, Hannah's scholarship was made possible by a bunch of teenagers.

For months, the civic-minded students did everything from baby-sitting to car-washing to come up with enough money to fund two scholarships. The first was given to one of the Mountain Scholars earlier in the evening. The second was the one for Hannah.

To many in the crowd, the teens' efforts were the highlight of the night.

As Greg's neighbor, Arthur, put it, "The Foundation had grown up in many ways, but at the end of the day, the name – 11-10-02 – represented the belief that people thirty and under could make a difference, too. Knowing that a bunch of students funded this final scholarship, I think it brought the entire thing full circle. It was a very cool moment."

The teenagers who funded these scholarships were led by Alex. After serving on the Junior Scholarship Board and reading about the nominees, he wanted to do more than vote. So, with the help of some of his friends, he raised the money to fund a couple scholarships.

A native of the same town where Greg and Charlie were raised, Alex was a little bit like both men – but not identical to either of them.

On the one hand, Alex shared Charlie's pursuit of life on the fast track to financial success. He was headed to the Ivy Leagues in the fall, planned to get an MBA when he was done, fully expected to land a high-paying job down the road – and made no apologies for any of it. On the other hand, like Greg, he was determined to make a difference while he was young.

In the end, Alex was not solely following Charlie's path to corporate America nor was he solely following Greg's path into the community. Instead, he was carving out his own path somewhere in the middle.

In the process, Alex became a living reminder that you don't have to choose between pursuing your dreams and helping other people pursue theirs. You can do a little of both and be a lot more balanced.

(29) If you want to conquer the world, you don't need to be 100% Charlie. If you want to help the world, you don't need to be 100% Greg. There is a middle ground. Find it.

With all the scholarships given out, Cliff approached the podium to thank everyone for coming to the event. As he did, he noticed Greg making his way toward the podium for the first time all night.

History was about to repeat itself.

When he got to the podium, Greg said he was sorry for interrupting – but the co-hosts' scripts were once again apparently missing a page or two. According to his copy, the show was not over.

He said the first surprise up his sleeve was another live auction.

"The cruise, the trip and diamond auctioned off earlier were great," he said, "but the most valuable items of all, I saved them for last!"

The audience was abuzz with excitement. What could be even more valuable than a cruise, a trip and a diamond? Was it a safari? A new car?

Uh, not exactly.

It turned out to be the stitches of Elliott's foul ball.

Greg's ex-girlfriend, Sloane, recalled, "And, by the way, Greg wasn't even auctioning the whole baseball. Just the red, stringy stuff!"

The audience shook their heads, but Greg said he was serious. He said the story behind the foul ball symbolized believing in yourself and seizing opportunities. Now that the string from the ball was framed, he insisted it was art. Expensive art. Worth no less than $5,000.

The room rocked with laughter, but Greg did not care. He knew all he needed was one person to believe in his vision. Sure enough, one did.

"Five thousand dollars!" a complete stranger shouted.

The room was in shock. Five grand for the red string from a baseball? It seemed too good to be true. And yet, Greg was only getting warmed up.

"We have one other outstanding item to auction!" he bellowed.

Outstanding? Um, *outlandish* might be a better way to put it.

The second item up for auction was a framed scrap of aluminum.

Guy, the photographer, laughed, "It was the flip-top from Greg's soda can. The one I used to get that camera to work. He kept it and framed it!"

Again, the audience laughed. The thing was garbage. Actual garbage. Again, Greg was unfazed by the reaction. He knew that one man's trash was another man's art. He knew all he needed was one person out of 500 to agree with him.

And, yet again, one person did.

One of the business executives who served on one of the Scholarship Boards bid $8,000! *For a piece of aluminum!*

The generous gift was the largest one-time donation the Foundation ever accepted.

It seemed to be a fitting finale to the Gala. A reminder that people will support your dreams if you believe in them enough.

But Greg was not done yet.

With the success of the auction, his confidence soared. He knew it was the perfect time to make the *really* big announcement – the one he waited for more than a decade to make.

"I have a dream!" Greg declared.

The audience giggled when they heard such famous words coming out of the mouth of the man with the mismatched socks, but Greg didn't laugh with them. This was, after all, *The Dream*. The one hatched inside his mind while sitting on a mattress in a dormitory hallway in Louisiana, with the poster of Dr. King over his shoulder.

What exactly was it? What was this *Dream* Greg held dear – and kept secret – for so many years?

He said his Dream was much like Dr. King's Dream. A world of people of different races and cultures coming together – with one slight twist.

In Greg's Dream, everyone was drinking milkshakes.

The audience laughed again, but he insisted he was serious.

His *Dream* was to bring the world together for milkshakes.

And he wanted everyone in the audience at the Gala to be part of it.

"And that's not all," he declared. "As we make the walk to get shakes, I want you to talk to people you don't already know. I want you to make new friends while we cross the street and get shakes."

Hannah later laughed, "It was the craziest thing I ever heard. He wanted everybody to get up and leave the hotel right then and right there."

It sounded crazy, indeed – except that, people did it.

Hundreds of people in suits and dresses. White, Black, Hispanic, Asian, young, old, educators and executives. They rose from their seats, followed Greg out of the ballroom, down the hall, out the door of The Big Hotel and across the street to a little milkshake shop. Along the way, they talked to the people walking on their left and on their right – even if they didn't know each other.

It was *exactly* as Greg dreamed.

As the night came to an end and people made their way home from the milkshake shop, Charlie approached his friend of twenty-five years and said, "It's not exactly how they taught me to do it in business school, but I have to admit, you had a vision and you made it come to life."

Greg smiled warmly. To hear Charlie acknowledge his way of doing things had value, too – to hear him admit there was more than one path to success – meant a lot to the entrepreneurial kid with no corner office.

Before Greg could say thanks, Charlie spoke again.

"There is one thing I don't get. If the shakes were so important, why not just have them delivered to us at the hotel? That would've been a lot easier."

Greg smiled and said, "Because it wasn't about milkshakes."

"But I thought you said – "

"It was about the walk, Charlie. It's always about the walk."

And that, indeed, was the moral of Greg's journey. The moral it took him nearly thirty years to understand. Whether you're trying to build a company, earn a degree or get a milkshake, it's the process of getting where you want to go that matters most. That's when you learn things – on your way to getting where you want to go. It's not about where you go or what you get when you arrive that is of greatest importance.

It's the walk – always the walk – that matters most.

**

Now that Greg brought the streak of brunches full circle, helped send thirty students to college and realized the beginning of his *Dream*, some people suggested he take what little time was left until his thirtieth birthday to finally relax a little and take a much-deserved vacation.

Greg appreciated the thought, but he had a different idea in mind. Instead of coasting to the finish line, he wanted to use the weeks that remained to test the limits of everything he learned over the previous twenty-nine years and eight months of his life.

And he knew exactly how he wanted to do it.

Over and over again, Greg was told the most important parts of his life were not real. His friends from his childhood backyard were not real. The people he admired in books and films were just characters. The thirty dreams on his Idea List were unrealistic. He wasn't a real student at VFWU. The cynics accused him of having muscles that were artificial. His room with the Lunch Lady was not a real office. His milkshake glasses were not real trophies. The event at The Restaurant was not really a Gala. The things he auctioned off were not real art. The degree from PSC was honorary. Even the competition that declared his Grandma to be the world's greatest was called a farce.

For nearly thirty years, he heard the doubters say these things. And for nearly thirty years, he tried to prove them wrong. But now, he had a different goal in mind.

Instead of convincing people something was real, could he convince them to believe in something that even he confirmed was not? Could he convince people to see the value in something that really didn't exist? Could he convince them to see value in *nothing*?

To find out the answer, he said he was going to create a film premiere from scratch. He planned to line up a caterer and get posters made. There would be newspaper ads and a billboard, too. And he vowed to get all the companies involved to do their parts for free.

It seemed like a difficult task, but there was an added wrinkle that seemed to make it downright impossible. *There was no film.*

Greg's friends insisted he was nuts. They said no company in its right mind supports the premiere of a film that does not actually exist.

Greg disagreed. He said it didn't matter if there was a film. He said if a person believed in something strongly enough, then others would believe in it, too – even if they knew it didn't exist.

He pushed ahead with his plan and called an executive to ask for his company's support.

"Wait a second," said the CEO. "I don't get it. No film?"

"That's right," Greg said proudly. "There's no film. Not even a short one. There's zilch, nada, nothing! So whaddya say? Are you in?!"

Not surprisingly, the CEO said no, and he wasn't alone.

Each time, Grandma's words – *keep failing until you succeed* – echoed in his head. He shrugged off the rejection and made more calls.

Within a few days, his persistence produced the results he wanted.

A top photographer named Vincent and a top graphic designer named Maria agreed to help Greg make the movie posters. A company agreed to print hundreds of copies once they were done. Another company agreed to put up a billboard right in the middle of town. The local paper agreed to run ads in the movie section to promote the event.

For the reception taking place at the 'premiere', Greg lined up companies to cater food and sodas for the hundreds of guests. Another company signed on to provide attendees with dessert – including the creation of a cheesecake in the shape of a giant milkshake.

And all of these folks agreed to do it for free.

Greg's friends were stunned, but they were positively speechless after discovering where the event was going to take place.

The movie theater.

Greg convinced its management to close part of the theater for one night – the night of his thirtieth birthday – to host the premiere of a film they knew did not exist. For the eight weeks leading up to the event, they even agreed to put the posters up in two dozen of their theaters right alongside the posters promoting real movies.

It all seemed too good to be true, but Greg was still not satisfied. His non-existent movie's premiere needed an audience!

In a speech before several hundred supporters, Greg announced the news about the big event at the movie theater on his thirtieth birthday.

Everyone seemed very excited. Then, he told them about the one small catch. It was going to be the premiere of a film that didn't actually exist. The audience was amused and confused all at once.

Elliott said, "The reception with the stars at the premiere sounded cool, except that, well, if there's no actual movie, then who are the stars?"

The whole thing seemed absurd, but there was no telling Greg that. In fact, he said the event was *so* special that tickets cost $125!

Arthur laughed, "This was the premiere of a film that did not exist. He would be lucky if people agreed to show up for free. To charge people $125 to go? He completely lost his marbles."

Arthur wasn't the only one who felt that way, but Greg didn't care one bit. He was certain that as long as he kept believing in his idea strongly enough, then other people eventually would, too.

Sure enough, they did. Slowly but surely, people filled out forms to buy tickets. In some cases, they bought as many as ten!

A local parent, Annie, one of the few who always told him to keep chasing his dreams, loved every second of it. She said, "It wasn't like he tricked anyone. They all knew there was no movie. And yet, they still ordered tickets to the premiere."

It seemed like Greg proved his inspiring point, but he had a bigger vision in mind. Having now convinced all these companies and people to see value in nothing, he wanted to do what he always dreamed. He wanted to make nothing become real. The godson of the local projectionist wanted to make that dark wall in the theater come to life.

"What do you mean?" Charlie asked.

With tears in his eyes, Greg hollered, "I'm making a movie!!"

**

His goal was to make a movie that could be shown at the premiere party taking place on the night of his thirtieth birthday.

The idea seemed to be Greg's nuttiest yet. He had 100 days to learn how to make a movie, come up with the equipment, write a script, assemble a cast, shoot the footage and have it edited and ready to play.

To avoid wasting any of his limited time doing research on some unknown subject, Greg decided to base the film on part of a story he already knew well – his own – but it hardly seemed to matter. Even if he had a good handle on the subject, it seemed impossible for a novice to make a movie in such a short period of time.

Greg assured his friends that it would all work out in the end. After all, Roy Hobbs didn't try out for pro baseball until he was much older.

"Who?" Charlie asked.

"You know," Greg said, "Roy Hobbs. The guy in *The Natural*. He was going to be a pro ballplayer, but he got sidetracked and didn't get the chance to chase his dream until he was older. Just like me and making movies. I was going to do it when I was younger, but I got sidetracked."

Charlie was tempted to point out the obvious – Hobbs wasn't real. He was just a character in a film. – but he knew it would be of no use.

And so it was, with a make-believe baseball player as his inspiration, Greg embarked on the project of a lifetime. He had to learn how to make a movie and then make one from scratch – all in 100 days.

And after all that work, he only planned on showing the finished product one time.

Greg said that one day, perhaps, he would tell the story of the first thirty years of his life. Maybe, *that* film or book would be seen or read around the world. But, the material he created over the next 100 days and nights was only going to be a "rough draft" of a portion of the story. And it was only going to be aired one time – the night of 11-10-02.

His friends couldn't understand the point of putting so much time and effort into something that only would be seen once and by so few people.

Greg always replied, "Because it's the walk that matters most."

In the days that followed, despite his inexperience, Greg got off to an impressive start. He managed to talk his way into film and cameras and access to a top-of-the-line studio where real productions were filmed. He also got two of his friends to help out with the editing. He lined up an entire 'cast', too. His friends, his students, the Lunch Lady, the restaurant managers – they all offered to take a turn in front of the camera.

As for Greg, he was having the time of his life. He practiced his 'Director' lines everywhere he went.

"Quiet on the set!" he hollered as he walked down the street.

"Action!" he blurted out in an elevator filled with strangers.

He even got his very own Director's Chair (Rocky, the kid in the tux, wrote *Director* on a piece of tape, stuck it on the back of a stool, smiled and said, "If it's a film to you, it's a film to me.")

Unfortunately, Greg's directorial honeymoon did not last long. His path always seemed to be riddled with roadblocks. These last hundred days until 11-10-02 were no different.

The first day on the set, he nearly started a fire. Then, a camera temporarily disappeared. One day, an entire box of tapes was misplaced. The editing machine broke down twice. For three days, Greg filmed people without realizing he failed to turn on their microphone.

And that's what happened on the set.

Off the set, Greg's path was no straight line, either. One day, a truck rammed into his car. A few weeks later, he gave a speech on the East Coast. After the event, the driver took him to the wrong airport, stranding him a thousand miles from home. His apartment got so cluttered with boxes that he ran out of space to sleep. More than once, he slept beneath the counter at a local 24 hour store. He stubbornly skipped meals to carve out extra time to complete the movie. With fifty days to go, he already lost nine pounds.

As always, he also had to endure the doubters.

"You have no business making movies. You ought to stick to helping kids," said one so-called 'expert' who Greg tried to contact for help.

As the date drew near, things went from bad to worse.

With less than thirty days to go until 11-10-02, Little Jarrett died. His brave friend from Kentucky finally lost his fight with cancer.

Despite all the setbacks and the grief – and despite not having his Grandma to call for advice any more – Greg refused to quit. He was determined to make his vision a reality.

From time to time, the stress got the best of him and he fired off another angry, rambling note. More often than not, though, the lessons of the past thirty years – lessons about teamwork and perspective – carried the day.

To make sure he stopped losing track of equipment (let alone nearly setting it on fire), Greg brought in a top film student to assist him. When the editing machine kept jamming, he turned to a top-level production company to lend a hand. Instead of giving up because some people wouldn't teach him anything, he found others who would.

No matter what happened, Greg rolled with the punches and stayed focused on his goal. Eventually, it all paid off. On the 98th night, he completed his task. He stuck the finished tape in an empty cereal box, headed home and waited for the big night to arrive.

The Movie Theater – November 10, 2002

With the name of Greg's one-night-only film up on the marquee, his friends and students streamed into the theater where they enjoyed the reception with the 'stars' of the film – *themselves.*

Elliott laughed, "The kids all wore dark shades and signed autographs. The adults did, too. For one night, we all felt like stars."

At precisely seven-thirty, with popcorn in one hand and soda in the other, the audience took their seats. A few moments later, the lights went out and the 'film' played.

A critic would say what was shown that night was not very good, and that critic would be right. By any standard, it was an amateur production. A rough draft pieced together in less than a hundred days by a guy who didn't know what he was doing, with a cast that had little idea how to act.

But the audience didn't seem to care, and neither did Greg. On that night, if only for one night, he did what he always dreamed since he was a boy in grade school visiting his godfather at the movie theater.

He made the wall come to life.

In the process, he told the kind of story he always vowed to tell.

A story about underdogs. About someone who stuck up for people who were treated differently. About a world where it's okay to dream.

Best of all, thanks to the sponsors and all those ticket sales, the event raised more money for the Foundation than any other night ever had.

In every sense, the night was perfect. The ultimate way to spend the final night of this thirty year journey. Two minutes into the film, Greg already had tears running down both cheeks.

After the final credits rolled, the Principal of Blue Academy walked to the front, took the microphone and introduced himself.

For the next few minutes, Mr. Brooks told the audience about Greg's efforts to help his school, his staff and his students over the years.

He said he knew Greg sacrificed his own dreams along the way to do it. He explained that the school was a small one in an economically challenged part of town. There wasn't much they could afford to do over the years to express the full extent of their gratitude.

Until now.

Mr. Brooks said there was a special way they could say thanks to Greg on this special night. He said he heard one of Greg's most deeply held dreams was to win "an Academy Award" for his first film.

"And," he said, "that is a dream we can help make come true."

At first, nobody seemed too sure what Mr. Brooks meant.

Then, he smiled and said, "Because, you know, as the Principal of Blue Academy, I am, technically speaking, the head of *an Academy*."

He paused for a moment to let his words sink in.

Then, he cleared his throat, smiled one more time and said, "Without further adieu, it's my pleasure to present the *Blue Academy* Award for Best Director of a Film That Does Not Yet Exist."

As the audience laughed and applauded, the substitute teacher-turned-movie director for one night walked down to the front of the theater and accepted the trophy.

It was a milkshake glass painted gold by the kids.

As Greg looked out at the crowd giving him a standing ovation, he noticed his mother, father and sister leading the applause.

His road had been so up-and-down over the years. He walked away from the kind of salary and certain future that parents usually want for their

92

child. But, in the end, his family knew this was his dream. Even if they didn't understand it, they wanted to see him achieve it and be happy.

With tears in his eyes, Greg raised up his gold trophy and gave an acceptance speech whose first six words he practiced all his life.

"I'd like to thank the Academy…"

(30) Stick with a dream long enough, and it just might come true.

After the crowd went home, Greg headed over to Tempo Cafe.

As he walked in, the manager smiled and said, "How'd the movie go?" Greg smiled back and said, "It went well, thanks."

Then, he joined me in the booth by the window, set down his lunchbox briefcase and gold milkshake glass trophy, took his shoes off his forever sore feet and ordered the same thing he ordered most of his life – a grilled cheese sandwich and a vanilla shake.

As the clock struck twelve and 11-10-02 came to an end, Greg began to tell me the story of the first thirty years of his life.

The dreams he had. The goals he set. The books he read. The movies he loved. The teachers he admired. The rejections he faced. The mistakes he made. The obstacles he overcame. The kids he taught, and the ones who taught him. The friends he found, and the ones he lost. His experiences, his decisions, his sacrifices, his impact. And above all else, a sense of what he learned during his memorable journey.

Because, as it turned out, The First Thirty didn't only refer to the first thirty years of his life, the first thirty goals on his Idea List, and the first thirty scholars he helped send to college. It also referred to the first thirty lessons learned from his setbacks and successes along the way.

**

I asked Greg one question: *Can you start at the beginning?*

By the time he finished his answer, it was now well past five o'clock in the morning. The late-night crowd at the cafe had long since left. The early risers had not yet arrived. In fact, there was only one other customer present – a woman, probably in her mid-forties, sitting in the booth right next to us.

As I packed up my things, I apologized to Greg for asking a question whose answer required so much of his time.

He laughed and said, "Don't worry about it. I've watched the sun rise more than once over the last few years."

You might think he was being polite, but he really didn't seem to mind the length of our meeting. In fact, at some point, after he finished the shake and the cheese sandwich, he had opened his lunchbox, pulled out a pencil and paper, and started to draw a picture of me while he told his story.

Every so often, he looked up at me – studying my face intently, double-checking every crease, every shadow – before turning his attention back to that paper and getting lost in the details of his artwork while simultaneously telling me about one chapter of his life after another.

Until, finally, hours later, he finished two portraits at once.

The picture of his life that he painted with his words, and the picture of me that he drew with his pencil.

I thanked him again for the chance to tell his story in a book. I promised to do my best to tell it well.

"I know you will," he said. "I always have believed in you."

With that, he put a tip on the table, tucked the paper and pencil back into his lunchbox briefcase, slipped on his shoes, picked up his golden trophy, rose from his seat, wished me well and turned to leave.

As he did, the lady next to us waved and said, "You too."

"Excuse me?" Greg responded politely.

"You said *take care of yourself*. There's nobody else here. So, even though you were looking out the window, I assumed you were talking to me. So, I was saying *you, too*."

The woman was trying to be nice, but I didn't think Greg was going to take it that way. When we were little and people said they didn't see me, he launched into a tantrum loud enough to wake up the neighbors.

But, on this particular night, he didn't get upset at all. In fact, he didn't even correct the other customer. To the contrary, he smiled, thanked her, and headed out the door.

Yesterday, if you told me that would be his reaction, I wouldn't have believed you. But now that I know where life has taken Greg in the twenty-five years since I last saw him, I'm not surprised at all.

If there's one thing he learned from his own story, it is that those who dare to pursue a dream will always encounter a person or two who don't see their vision.

If you have a positive dream and good intentions, I hope you remember that and don't get discouraged by those who doubt you. Anything your mind can think of – a friendship, a foundation, a film – can become a reality if you're willing to spend the time it takes to make it come to life.

Imaginary doesn't mean something doesn't exist.

It means something doesn't exist *yet*.

It is okay to dream.

And if you try to make your dream come to life like Greg did, and you run into a few obstacles along the way like he did, I hope you'll remember what his Grandma always said:

If life was nothing but straight lines, it wouldn't be worth living.

**

AFTER THOUGHTS

The next year, the Foundation had another Gala.
It took place back at The Restaurant.

Greg eventually raised the 'price' of his milkshakes to $10,000 each.
To justify the increased cost, he added one final ingredient which he said
captured the true essence of his Foundation. A single nut on top.

More than 20 years since its start, The 11-10-02 Foundation continues to
provide grants and scholarships to students around the country.

To this day, Greg has still never accepted a salary for running it.

Greg's portraits have been exhibited at events in different countries.
The collection is called *My Sleepless Nights*.

He frequently speaks at schools, organizations, companies and conferences.

In 2005, he was invited to give a speech at Princeton University.
It was the first time he ever set foot on an Ivy League campus.
After he spoke, he was honored for his efforts as a 'social entrepreneur'.
When the event was over, he went for a walk to get a milkshake.
The people in attendance got up and went with him.

He still wears mismatched socks.

Pick up a pen – fill out this page – and make this book your own

My first name is: _____

Today's Date is: _____ - _____ - _____

Of all the lessons shared in this story, my favorite is number _____ .

Pick one of the next two lines and fill out this section

Under 30. My '11-10-02' (my 30th b-day) is: _____ - _____ -_____

Over 30. My next '11-10-02' (my 60th/90th b-day) is: _____ - _____ -_____

Here's a list of three things I hope to accomplish by that date:
1. _____
2. _____
3. _____

An issue that is important to me: _____

_____

One positive, safe way I can be 'more than a bystander' and get more involved in addressing that issue: _____

_____
_____

*Pick a window you look out on a regular basis –
such as a bedroom window, classroom window or office window.*

When I look out my window, I see: _____

_____
_____

I could improve the world outside my window if I: _____

_____
_____
_____

There are other versions of this story for audiences of different ages & reading levels – as well as – a companion journal workbook based on this story. For more on those books and that workbook, visit

www.GregForbes.com/books